THE TRADITIONAL DANCE

SPANISH BASQUE STICK DANCERS

From a gouache by Ramiro Arrue

THE TRADITIONAL DANCE

by

VIOLET ALFORD

AUTHOR OF 'ENGLISH FOLK DANCES'

and

RODNEY GALLOP

AUTHOR OF 'A BOOK OF THE BASQUES'

With 14 Illustrations

METHUEN & CO. LTD. LONDON

36 Essex Street W.C.2

First published in 1935

PRINTED IN GREAT BRITAIN

PREFACE

IN this book we have attempted a general survey of the traditional dances of Europe and the British Isles, to coincide with the International Folk Dance Festival, London, July 1935. Wherever possible our account of this fascinating by-way where art and custom meet is based on personal observation. We do not claim for one moment to have included every dance in Europe, nor even every type of dance, for this would have been wearisome to the reader and impossible in the space at our disposal. The principal types, however, are all included and sorted into their proper categories in such a way as will, we hope, prove helpful to those who see them, whether in London on this unique occasion, or in their native countries. Our aim, therefore, has been to make the book representative rather than encyclopedic, and we have tried, moreover, to describe only the best of each type.

For the convenience of the general reader references and footnotes have been reduced to a minimum.

V.A.
R.A.G.

CONTENTS

CHAPTER IV

'RING-A-RING O' ROSES'

CHAPTER V

'THREE MEET'

CHAPTER VI

CHRISTIANS AND MOORS

CHAPTER VII

'LONG WOODEN IDOLS'

CHAPTER VIII

HORNS, HOOFS AND FEATHERED FOWLS

CHAPTER IX

RELIGIOUS DANCES

CHAPTER X

'A GREEN STAGE'

ILLUSTRATIONS

INTRODUCTION

THE FOOL SPEAKS

'I am the Clown of this noble town
And I've comed to see thee dance.'
(*Mummers' Play*)

'NOBODY like us!' cries the Fool of the Valles Gipsy Dance, slashing the legs of his rivals with his whip as his company dances on to the village square.

'*Ningú com nosaltres*,' is his Catalan cry.

So they all say, those bands of peasant folk, who from one end of Europe to the other maintain their traditional dance. You find them everywhere, in remote mountain villages as in unexpected corners of busy towns, in Oxfordshire as in the Balkans, and wherever they are, of whatever race or creed, the one thing you may be certain of is that they will claim uniquity.

'Nobody like us,' they cry.

They are wrong, of course. But they are not in a position to know how far wrong, for it is only those able to go and see for themselves who are capable of judging that.

Travel and patient investigation alone will supply the necessary comparative knowledge. Even when the means of comparison have been painfully acquired a standard will be found necessary, a norm to which one may turn and say, this dance, degenerate, unbeautiful, falls short of it; that other, traditionally pure, a thing of both interest and beauty, goes far beyond it; a third attains it and no more. This standard we have in our own country, and for the rapid tour of Europe we are about to undertake we can choose no better starting-point than England, who possesses in her own dances every variety needed with which to compare continental examples of the art.

Not that for one moment, with misguided insularity, we would cry, 'Nobody like us!' But our store is better than many, inferior to some, handier than any as a standard of comparison. So we set it up like a signpost at a place where three ways meet. One arm points to a snowy landscape and says, 'Mummers and Sword dances'.

The second is marked 'Morris', and indicates a lane green with the greenery of May.

The third, marked 'Country dances', points to no lane at all, but to a long hall lit with candles and lined with red rout seats. But at the end of it we see through an open window a tall Maypole with a rowdy throng about it, farther off people stepping

Hornpipes, Jigs and Reels to the sound of the Irish pipes, and beyond again, on short Scottish turf, men treading Strathspeys, Reels and swaggering solos, swinging their kilts like the skirts of a ballerina.

To winter and Whitsuntide we can return in the proper place; let us then first walk into the candle-light.

CHAPTER I

'ALL IN A ROW'

'Begin,' says Hal, 'Aye, aye,' says Mall,
'We'll lead up Packington's Pound';
'No, no,' says Noll and so says Doll,
'We'll first have Sellenger's Round.'
(*Come Lassies and Lads*)

A BALLROOM seems an unsuitable setting for Country dances. But the name is probably a mistake for 'counter', as in the French *Contre-danse*, which is itself a Country dance, so that an old-fashioned, or for that matter a modern ballroom is a perfectly proper place for them. These are not ceremonial dances fixed to the festal calendar, but recreational and social dances that any one can do who takes the trouble to remember the figures, or is quick enough to copy them. The curious thing is not that they were once fashionable, but that they ever fell out of fashion. In the eighteenth century ball programmes consisted of Minuets first and

Country dances afterwards. When the Valse came in Minuets went out, but not Country dances. When the Quadrille came in these three went on together, amusingly enough, for the 'new' French Quadrille was nothing but an English square Country dance returned home under a new name. Then the Polka and all the other dances for couples poured in, and soon of the old social Country dances only *Sir Roger de Coverley* remained. Why just this one it is hard to say, for it is neither particularly amusing nor beautiful. Country fashion, however, lags behind the times, and Country dances went on for a long while, oblivious to the fact that they were no longer 'the thing'. I often danced them at a Somerset Harvest Home, the gentlemen touching their forelocks every time they met their ladies in the figure. For in the Harvest Home tent we were all genteel. It remained for the present revival to turn us into mere men and women.

There are several forms of Country dance. The oldest and simplest is the Round, a descendant of the medieval *Carole,* a singing dance which gave its name to Carols, Christmas and otherwise. The Carol was not used entirely for pleasure, but was also a ritual dance, as when wassailing a fruit tree to make it bear, or round a Maypole to magic in the spring. It began, one supposes, on the circular dancing floors of ancient Greece, and is done to-day on Navarrese threshing floors, and it melts naturally into that archaic form, the Chain dance, when the latter breaks into a single file. We catch glimpses of it in its prime, chiefly through ecclesiastical censure, to which indeed we owe most of our knowledge of the amusements of the common folk—so great a dread of dancing had Mother Church. That old book of morality, *Handlynge Sinne*, sounds as though it were from a Puritan pen, though in reality it dates from 1303. The author writes of

> daunces, Carols and Somour games,
> of many swych come many shames,

and deplores the habit of borrowing finery

> yn Carol to go.

We possess a dance tune of about that date, nine bars instead of the modern eight in each part, but eminently danceable, and it might well belong to a Carol in transition between sung and instrumental accompaniment. When the Carol grew into a round Country dance it almost invariably took the name of the tune to which it was done, and to which it had perhaps been sung. These were ballad tunes—whence the French *ballader*, *balladin* and all derivatives, including, of course, the all-comprising *ballet*, with its music, *décor*, declamation and dance. We find no Carols after the fifteenth century; already at the very opening of the sixteenth it had changed to the Round, and at the first marriage of Catherine of Aragon in 1501 'goodly roundels and other figures were performed in a masque'. One of the earliest we know by name is *Sellenger's Round,* while in Scotland in 1548, Lowland shepherds were seen 'to dance in a ring; every old shepherd led his wife by the hand, and every young shepherd her whom he loveth best'.

From the Round developed the Square, and forms for three couples or four came in, the men facing the women; and if the dates of their tunes are any guide, early Tudor days saw *The Beggar Boy, Greenwood* with its lovely air, *Half Hannikin*—the tune to which some one long after wrote *Here's to the Maiden of Bashful Fifteen*—*The Hunt is Up*, and many others already in full popularity. *The Mery Ballet of the Hawthorne Tre*, or *Donkin Dargason,* is of the same period but of quite a different form, one long line, all the men facing one way, all the women the other, and its pattern is unique amongst our Country dances. Elizabeth's maids of honour, so fond of 'heying about', loved *Trenchmore* and the queer old *Cushion Dance,* finding them a grateful change from Court Pavanes, Courantes and Galliards. When Buckingham was prime favourite, his young brothers and sisters were laughed at for putting on fine clothes more easily than learning the dances *à la mode*, but the King arranged that 'only Country dances' should be done as they did not know the French ones. Charles II delighted in his native figures, and Pepys' well-known description is enlightening. He went to Court one evening and there saw first a *Branle*, then a *Coranto*. Then the King called for a Country dance which he himself led, its inelegant name far too appropriate to that unbridled company. '*Cuckolds all Awry*,' said he, 'the dance of old England.'

This appears in the first edition of Playford's *Dancing Master* with a secondary title, *Hey Boys up go We*, which had been a Cavalier song. The Court had turned its back on *Old Noll's Jig* with a vengeance. About this time another form was developing with the engaging name of *Longways for as Many as Will*, the men facing the women as in *Sir Roger de Coverley*, and some of the earliest of these, like *Hey Boys*, were danced to Cavalier tunes, *Prince Rupert's March*, for instance, and the *Twenty-ninth of May*. From now on we are on firm ground with one edition after another of Playford's *Dancing Master* to give figures, dates and tunes. Between 1651 and 1728 this treasure store went through seventeen editions, and allows us to trace the change in fashion, for the first edition gives many Rounds and few Longways, the last all Longways but fourteen. In the country, however, the old forms went on, and we see Dorset folk in Hardy's *Under the Greenwood Tree* enjoying a hands-six-round well into the nineteenth century, while the Elizabethan *Cushion Dance*, long since forgotten at Court, lingered on in Cornish and Cotswold villages, its obligatory kissing, one suspects, having something to do with its length of life.

Still other dances were being used in the country up to about eighty years ago, and of these we seem to have lost all trace—at least of the Jig and the Hornpipe, for the third, the Reel, lives in Scotland, on the Border, and in Ireland. In England it only exists as a figure, the well-known *Hey*. The Jig and the Hornpipe have left but their name, and appear to have been very springy in the true English 'lofty manner'. Mrs. Pepys' maid Mercer, one remembers, danced a Jig in 'the most natural way of it', and the Misses Flamborough at the Vicar of Wakefield's gathering 'understood the jig and the roundabout to perfection, but were totally unacquainted with Country dances'. I take this to mean the Longways form, then very fashionable in other circles, too fashionable for these country girls, who clung to the round form. This perpetual interchange must always be taken into account, sometimes the country bringing fashions to town, as we saw when Buckingham's family, reversing the Misses Flamborough's dilemma, arrived understanding Country dances but totally unacquainted with the French ones, more often the town sending fashions into the country. Even Jigs and Hornpipes had once been fashionable too, as the names of the tunes (taken by Playford for his Country dance figures) tell us—*Lord of Carnarvon's Jig, Lady Banbury's Hornpipe,* and the Longways called after the famous tight-rope dancer, *Jacob Hall's Jig.* The Hornpipe was known to Ben Jonson and earlier still, and with the Jig was extraordinarily popular throughout the seventeenth century, developing at one time into an interlude, or 'sketch', with lines to speak as well as steps to dance, so that William Kemp, that Elizabethan actor who sought notoriety in dancing the Morris step from London to Norwich, and the Georgian dancer of old Sadler's Wells, Nancy Dawson, performed stage Jigs and Hornpipes before the Misses Flamborough had ever heard of them.

What these dances really were is difficult now to surmise. Originally in triple time they changed into common measure like the one well known as the *College Hornpipe,* and even the evergreen *Sir Roger* has been classified both as Jig and Hornpipe—while we should call them both Country dances. To-day none but the once fashionable Longways are to be found in villages, and very few of them in England, though traditional (as opposed to revived) Country dancing is quite lively in Scotland.

The pleasures of Country dancing cannot be appreciated through watching it. It must be done. How much pleasanter (and more amusing) than to slip, slip, slip with one partner round a ballroom is it to greet your acquaintances as you meet them in a Longways.

'Cold night, isn't it? Figure of eight now.'

You pass your helpful friend.

'Look at my partner! She has got over to the men's side somehow.'

'That's all right. This dance is "improper".'

And how much more exhilarating than the dreary treadmill of *Paul Jones* to be snatched away by some intruding male, your own trotting behind all alone; and how heartening to feel the communal pull and weight of a great swinging hands-all round, and how pleasing to give an ear—an accomplishment completely lost in present-day ballrooms—to the delicate old tunes as well as to their rhythm.

How did it come about that we began again to stand up in a row, and to lead down the dance? To begin at the beginning, Cecil Sharp, already at work on his folk-song collections, happened one long-ago day upon a Morris 'side'. They came from Headington, now almost a suburb of Oxford, and the story shall be taken from the life of the founder of the English Folk Dance Society, told there as he so often told it.

'On Boxing Day, as he was looking out of the window upon the snow-covered drive, a strange procession appeared: eight men dressed in white, decorated with ribbons, with pads of small latten-bells strapped to their shins, carrying coloured sticks and white handkerchiefs; accompanying them was a concertina-player and a man dressed as a "Fool". Six of the men formed up in front of the house in two lines of three; the concertina-player struck up an invigorating tune, the like of which Sharp had never heard before; the men jumped high into the air, then danced with springs and capers, waving and swinging the handkerchiefs which they held, one in each hand, while the bells marked the rhythm of the step. The dance was the now well-known Morris dance, *Laudnum Bunches*, a title which decidedly belies its character. Then, dropping their handkerchiefs and taking each a stick, they went through the ritual of *Bean Setting*. This was followed by *Constant Billy* (*Cease your Funning* of the *Beggar's Opera*), *Blue-eyed Stranger* and *Rigs o' Marlow*. Sharp watched and listened spellbound. He felt that a new world of beauty had been revealed to him. He had not been well; his eyes had been giving him pain, and he was still wearing a shade over them, but all his ills were forgotten in his excitement. He plied the men eagerly with questions. They apologized for being out at Christmas; they knew Whitsun was the proper time, but work was slack and they thought there would be no harm in earning an honest penny. The concertina-player was Mr. William Kimber, junior, a young man of twenty-seven, whose fame as a dancer has now spread all over England. Sharp noted the five tunes from him next day, and later on many more.

'In telling the story of the folk-music revival, Sharp always spoke of this Headington incident as the turning-point of his life. . . .'[1]

The whole combination of circumstances was not far short of miraculous, for who else but Cecil Sharp possessed the musicianship, the love of the folk and their arts, together with the ability to attack such an undertaking as the notation of intricate dances? Who else but Mr. Kimber so honoured his traditional inheritance, had the patience and the ability to impart it, and the understanding of the worth of what he was giving? More intelligent than the simple Basque musician, who on seeing his hereditary tunes in print, cried out in despair, 'They have taken my tunes to Pampeluna. This is the end of them!' he was proud to give them to others from his safe keeping. He it was who went to London to teach girls

[1] Reprinted from *Cecil Sharp*, by A. H. Fox-Strangways in collaboration with Maud Karpeles, by permission of the author and collaborator, and the Oxford University Press.

of the Working Girls' Esperance Club; they it was who supplied the first teachers to those already clamouring to be taught. The first time my eyes saw the result, my ears heard our gay, heartening tunes, something within me said, 'Nothing on earth shall stop me learning too. This is *ours*.'

So here, when it is English for the English, we can exclaim with all sincerity, 'Nobody like us.' Something wakes up within, and the jingle of *our* bells, the rhythmic sound of *our* feet, the clashing of *our* sticks carries us back to past generations of Morris dancers, and them forward to us, so that, as ever in stout old England, we join in one long line, and all together through the centuries 'in wavering Morrice move'. But new-comers flocked in, and the Morris —meant for robust men and learned with difficulty and patience—required seconding with something easier. Country dances stepped in, first a few Longways noted from villagers in places where they still danced them, then by handfuls, Rounds, Squares, all sorts, dipped from the lucky dip of Master John Playford's *Dancing Master*. Here again Cecil Sharp's ability was needed to decipher the old books, and make them intelligible to less patient people. Then with Sword, Morris and Country dances for a repertoire the English Folk Dance Society was formed, and grew till not a county but has its branch, hardly a town but has its centre. Then the Board of Education put their own songs and dances into the school children's time-table, the Scouts began to dance and the Girl Guides, the Women's Institutes and the Police. The Universities were in it from the beginning, Oxford first, Cambridge next, the Summer Schools began at Stratford-on-Avon, and far-off cousins from the States come to stare at Ann Hathaway's cottage, stared at us too, and felt the Call of the Blood, and presently began to dance across the water. In the early days of the revival the queerest things happened quite easily.

'Round. Catherine P. Scott,' appeared on a programme, and an excited lady in the audience was heard to exclaim: 'The next isn't an English dance at all, I heard them say *The American Seat*!'

It needed a moment to recognize *Gathering Peascods* and the slightly archaic title *The Merry Conceit*. And the memory of Retford's Mayor lightly leaping in white sweater and gold chain, and another of Cecil Sharp clapping hands with Marie Corelli, all pink net and rosebuds in *Sweet Kate*, remain with me; and that of an ardent young propagandist on the platform of a Women's Institute assuring her sedate audience that though Sword dances were for men, Country dances were recreational and sexual.

The war slowed down the tempo but took the dances into the Y.M.C.A. huts, and revivalists recognized their brothers by whistling *Getting Upstairs* or

Shepherds' Hey, as Esmond recognized the English company across the Rhine when he heard *Lilliburlero*. When the giver to England of all these good gifts left us, those who had been in it from the beginning trembled a little for the future. But as ever, with the need came the man: Douglas Kennedy stepped into the breach, Maud Karpeles and Dr. Vaughan Williams seconding, everybody put their shoulders to the wheel and the first All England Festival burst upon us. Up to London they came from the farthest corners of our island. The floor of London University Great Hall saw, and felt, the rhythm of the Helston Furry processional; traditional Sword dancers came from Northumbria, their little old accordionist bringing his little old wife with him; the Welsh marches were there and Somerset, Roman Bath and rural Essex, while William Kimber, the beginner of it all, danced his famous Morris Jig. We were astonished and we were proud. Things never looked back after that. The English Folk Dance Society amalgamated with the Folk Song Society; the home for both grew up—not indeed in a single night, for it cost a hard struggle—and to-day Cecil Sharp House decorates a corner of Regent's Park Road architecturally, and we think spiritually. People laugh at us of course, we pity them profoundly; criticisms are heard and often deserved. Ballet founded on folk dance is attempted, does not succeed yet, for the producers will not yet recognize the too visible fact that such enterprises go far beyond their technique, and that only those with some operatic ballet training can thus use a folk base.

Again the revival has, without one shadow of doubt, inculcated a style probably never seen before, and which certainly never belonged to Country dances. Throughout their whole history it is the sprightliness, the springs which struck onlookers.

> They did dance as in France,
> Not in the English lofty manner.

and a little later,

> She jumps as high as he,
> Oh, how they do spring it,
> flounce it and fling it,
> Under the greenwood tree.

And in ballrooms too. Anne Boleyn danced the English dances, 'leaping and jumping with infinite grace and agility', and Buckingham, to stop a show of temper on the part of James I, 'sprang forward, cutting a score of lofty and minute capers with much agility and grace', while an English Admiral, at the great ball at Valladolid given for that same crusty Majesty's Ambassador, 'caused much surprise by his leaps and cabriolets'. The dancing masters, Beau Nash and that long ballroom with the red rout seats subdued the lofty manner, and the revival teaches a real *terre-à-terre*. The Scottish style seems nearer the mark, though they perhaps make a mistake too in using Fling steps, for what have Highland step-dances to do with Lowland Country dance figures? To those who know the robust, spontaneous vitality of authentic traditional dancers, there does seem something anaemic in the too-studied movements of the revivalists. Probably it is a matter of self-consciousness, that curse of modern life.

No matter. Let us enjoy the giddy corkscrew of *Strip the Willow*, to the tune of *Drops of Brandy* to render it still giddier, and having danced folk dances with the folk of many countries, I can still say that with plenty of room and a good musician

> There's none like a Country dance for pleasure.

CHAPTER II

I

GONE ABROAD

. . . They did dance
Into France,
Out of France, into Spain. . . .
(*Nursery Rhyme*)

IN every country in Europe the traditional dance is still very much alive. Like all living things, however, it is subject to the laws of change and growth. In the preceding chapter we have seen the gradual evolution of the Country dance in our own land through the centuries. We have seen, too, that like the living thing it is, it does not stand still in place any more than it does in time. Like other arts the dance knows no frontiers, and like many another fashion it is carried from one country to another, and adopted by people who had no part in its creation.

Thus Holland, a land in which the countryside has always tended, more even than elsewhere, to model itself on the middle classes of the towns, owes some of its dances to France, the setter of so many fashions, and others to England, and has been unable to develop them into anything distinctly Dutch. In the seventeenth century the Dutch, like every one else, danced in their ballrooms Low Dances, Branles and Alamandes, as to-day they dance *Anna van Duinen*, which is not, as you might think, the name of a local beauty, but a corruption of a Quadrille figure, *en avant deux*. On one island Dutch fishermen still dance an English Reel, and call it by its English name.

English Country dance tunes appear frequently in Dutch (as in German and Danish) collections as early as 1626, 1634 and 1648. On the title-page of the best known of these, that of the poet Starter, is an engraving showing two couples standing as for our English Country dance *Rufty-Tufty*. The sober Dutch slowed down our spirited tunes, however, and, as Dr. Elise van der Ven-ten Bensel has shown, our lively *Cushion Dance, Hit and Miss* and *Cobbler's Jig* appear in their collections as hymns in praise of the Lord, or of the Prince of Orange or other historical personages.

Whether or not we really invented the Country dance, our claim to have done so has been generally recognized, and we certainly made it more specially our own, and contributed more than any one else to its development and elaboration. In his *Recueil de Contre-danses* (1707) Feuillet says that the English were the 'first inventors' of the Country dance, and we can recognize our own *Greensleeves* in his *Les Manches Vertes.* Six years later Weaver writes in his *History of Dancing,* that 'Country dances are a dancing the peculiar growth of this nation, though now transplanted into almost all the Courts of Europe'. In Florence in 1740 Walpole exclaims, that 'Italians are fond to a degree of our Country dances', and about the same time the Romans were enjoying our *Buttered Pease* as *Piselli al Burro.* A century later the amusing writer who concealed his identity under the initials A.P.D.G. wrote in his *Sketches of Portuguese Manners and Customs* (1826), that 'in many societies, particularly in the provinces, the English Country dances are still in use'.

Since they passed from fashion in aristocratic ballrooms our Country dances have lost abroad their brevet of nationality, but their imprint may still be seen. Near Vianna do Castello, for instance, I was invited to see a Portuguese folk dance called *O Pretinho—The Little Nigger Boy.* It proved to be identical with *Strip the Willow.* Similarly the *Sekstur,* still popular in Norway, is a purely English Country dance, and the *Virginian Reel* of the United

States is none other than our old friend *Sir Roger de Coverley*.

It is an enthralling pursuit to trace the passage of these migratory birds of dance and song, and one which leads to fascinating discoveries. One romantic find was in the North American Appalachian Mountains, where English traditional songs and dances came to light, many of which had long since been forgotten in the Mother Country. In this long chain of mountains, stretching from the Canadian border in the north to Alabama in the south, there live scattered communities of people known to the cities as 'mountain whites', or 'poor white trash'. Mostly illiterate and having no money (they are self-supporting except for barter) they live in very primitive conditions in remote valleys or 'creeks' with names evocative of the Wild West, such as Possum Trot, Dish Rag, Kingdom Come, Hell for Sartin and Devil's Fork, this last renamed Sweet Water by the missionaries.

Doubtless because of their illiteracy and isolation they have been branded as degenerates, and much has been written by sensation-mongers about their family blood-feuds and their illicit stills, but Cecil Sharp found them 'just English peasants in appearance, speech and manners', or rather 'just exactly what the English peasant was one hundred or more years ago'.

'They have an easy, unaffected bearing,' he particularizes, 'and the unself-conscious manners of the well-bred. . . . Physically they are strong and of good stature, though usually spare in figure. Their features are clean-cut and often handsome; while their complexions testify to wholesome, out-of-door habits. . . .'

Among these people, cut off from outside influences, Cecil Sharp and Maud Karpeles found traditional songs and dances preserved ever since their ancestors emigrated from the Mother Country. 'Practically all the songs and ballads can be traced to English or Lowland-Scottish sources,' writes Miss Karpeles, 'but the tunes are very different in character from those which have been noted in this country in recent times. Whether they have suffered a sea-change, or whether they represent English folk-music of an earlier period is open to argument.' It is by no means impossible that these songs are purer and more faithful to tradition than those recorded at home, for this is certainly the case in the communities of Jews expelled from Spain as long ago as 1492, who are to-day scattered over the Levant, and who have preserved Spanish ballads which no longer survive in the Peninsula, and which, moreover, they pronounce with the accent not of the twentieth century, but of the Middle Ages.

CARINTHIAN LÄNDLER, AUSTRIA (*above*)

A GOTA: A PORTUGUESE COUNTRY DANCE FROM CARREÇO, NEAR VIANA DO CASTELO (*below*)

Curiously enough 'set-running', which is the only form of Appalachian Country dance (though Square dance figures survive in Northern New York State), is one that has nowhere been recorded in the United Kingdom. And a thrilling, breath-taking performance it is, as any will admit who have seen it perfectly 'run' by the Demonstration Team of the English Folk Dance and Song Society.

Let us hear Sharp's own description of it as he saw it for the first time:

'It was danced one evening after dark on the porch of one of the largest houses of the Pine Mountain School, with only one dim lantern to light up the scene. But the moon streamed fitfully in, lighting up the mountain peaks in the background and, casting its mysterious light over the proceedings, seemed to exaggerate the wildness and the breakneck speed of the dance. There was no music, only the stamping and clapping of the onlookers, but when one of the emotional crises of the dance was reached . . . the air seemed literally to pulsate with the rhythm of the "patters" and the tramp of the dancers' feet, while, over and above it all, floated the even, falsetto tones of the Caller, calmly and unexcitedly reciting his directions.'[1]

[1] Reproduced by kind permission of Messrs. Novello from *The Country Dance Book*, Part V, pp. 14, 15.

All through northern, western and central Europe we may follow the Country dance, which on the Continent has often borrowed from children's games ingenuous little hand-clappings, finger-waggings, bowings, kissings, and chuckings under the chin, as in the Dutch *Drickusman,* of which not only the steps and figures but words and music reappear almost unaltered in the Swedish *Klappdans* and Bohemian *Judentans.* Like bread upon the waters there has returned to us from Scandinavia that *Swedish Dance,* a Longways, which with *Sir Roger de Coverley* shared the honours of our children's parties.

Country dance figures are found as far east as Latvia, where they are dignified with exotic names such as *Ackups, Sudmalinas* and *Jandalins.* Another outpost of the Country dance is Austria. From Vienna, Lady Mary Wortley Montagu wrote in 1717: 'The Ball always concludes with English Country dances to the number of thirty or forty couples, and so ill danced that there is little pleasure in them. They know but half a dozen, and they have danced them over and over these fifty years. I would fain have taught them some new ones, but I found it would be some months' labour to make them comprehend them.'

To-day, a more recent and extraneous influence has made itself felt on the Country dance in Austria. In spite of rustic names such as *Schwefelhölzl, Buama-schlag* and *Der paschade Flugs-ummi,* many of these are recognizably degenerate ballroom dances. If the peasants of Tyrol, Salzkammergut or Burgenland still dance in a ring, the ring is not made by linking hands, but is broken up into pairs, man and girl together, stepping out in rustic Polkas or Valses.

We will not discuss the question of how much the ballroom dance owes to the folk dance, and how far it repays this debt. The relation of folk art to sophisticated art is a contentious and profitless subject, for it resolves itself into something like the question of which came first, the hen or the egg. If some folk dances are obviously degenerate ballroom dances, the latter must originally have been elaborated out of folk dances, such as the real Polish Polka and the Germanic Ländler. If one goes back far enough, of course, one comes to a time when folk dance and art dance were one, for the simple reason that social distinctions were infinitely less wide than they are to-day.

II

'STEP AND FETCH HER'

Stand and face your lover,
Stand and face your lover,
Stand and face your lover
as you have done before.
(*Singing Game*)

The reason for dancing in couples is the reason that makes people go courting in couples, so the more primitive the dance the less the woman partner has to do, for it has always been man's prerogative to display his prowess before the lady. But dancing in couples to-day means slipping about a ballroom, and although the male partner has not much opportunity to show himself off, he does still manage to set the step, which the lady must follow.

Before the modern so-called 'round' dances for couples came in, which happened with the appearance of the Valse at the beginning of the nineteenth century, the man had grand opportunities for display, his lace frills, his embroidered waistcoats helping, as he 'made a leg' clad in a silk stocking, in the grave promenades of a Minuet. The spinning Valse, followed by the Gallop and the Polka, did away with all that, and we see Dicken's gentlemen, whiskers flying, ringleted ladies tightly embraced, dashing and hopping among the antimacassared furniture much to their own satisfaction. Some of these active nineteenth century dances, long since forgotten in ballrooms, still eke out an existence in far-away places, country people invariably claiming them as their own productions. French Catalans, for instance, adore the Gallop, the Pyrenean valley of Couserans dances the Schottisch, and both believe these were never danced elsewhere. This is one way of making a 'folk' dance. We have just seen how the reverse process makes a ballroom dance. But to see man in his proper place we must look at very different exhibitions from these.

A couple of stout peasant people step out from a gathering of other stout peasant people, a musician lays his zither on the table and plays over a tinkling, triple measure tune. We are under the great spreading roof of a brown chalet in the Canton of Bern, and all these comfortable-looking persons are a Swiss Choral Society, out for an evening's amusement and sing-song. Although no wedding is actually contemplated, one soon will be, for the dance preparing is the traditional wedding dance, the *Lauterbach*. The man takes his partner by the hand and walks her round, picking up a small Valse step as he goes, or a step and hop, the free foot swung across the stepping foot. He wears a black velvet coat with short puffed sleeves, from beneath which snowy white shirt-sleeves appear. Across his chest and round his waist are embroidered bands, glittering with silver cows, velvety edelweiss and glowing blue gentians. His partner is a picture in bright brocaded apron, black bodice with swinging silver chains and filigree bosses. Her black lace head-dress stands out like a halo round her ruddy, cheerful face. Now the man continues the same Valse step but *vis-à-vis*, after which another round of the room is made, he turning her under his arm, she spinning like a top, full skirts filling with wind and spreading like an umbrella. Then comes hand-clapping and a loving promenade, arms round necks, he miming the smoking of his curved Swiss pipe, she giving the ' glad eye ' in a manner unexpected in so solid a lady. Now comes the Invitation, he bowing, supplicating, she coldly refusing—until the last second, when they break into a flying Valse, she retreating, he pursuing, and helping her on too, by a firm hand on her firm waist. Finally he kneels—but it is ' all my eye and Betty Martin ', for he knows his conquest is made, she valses round him somewhat triumphantly, thinking no doubt that the conquest is hers, and off they go again linked in a complicated embrace, his left hand holding her right on high, his right hand holding her left crossed behind her back. And all the time the zither tinkles out the tune we once knew as *The Dutchman's Little Wee Dog*.

This coy courting dance seems likely enough to lead to the wedding to which it belongs, but in the Austrian Alps they would consider it altogether too bashful, for their version of it has developed into the most open display of male 'show-off' imaginable. The man turns somersaults before the lady, indulges in cartwheels, stands on his head, even rolls on the floor, not to mention slapping himself all over from his cheeks to the soles of his shoes. This amusing if crude exhibition, the Tyrolese *Schuhplattler*, is said to imitate the antics of the courting black-cock before the demure grey-hen. When there is a cock too many he will seize another man, turn him completely upside down so that the inverted legs of the one are imprisoned beneath the arms of the other, and thus promenade round the room, yodelling in full blast, and each half of these Siamese twins soundly dusting the breeches of the other.

Their Hungarian neighbours boast a pair dance, the *Czardas*, which certainly owes nothing to the ballroom although it has been successfully transplanted there. The man puts his hands round the girl's waist, and she lays hers on his shoulders. Thus embraced they do a simple *chassé* sideways on each foot alternately, slowly in the *lassan* section, quickly in the *fris*. This is all the basic step, but the virtuosity of the dancers embellishes it with the most complex and elaborate variations. As danced by the gaily dressed peasants of the great plains of Hungary, it is an exhilarating sight, to which the passionate music in syncopated rhythm of the gipsy orchestra lends a peculiarly exciting quality.

Norway again shows the *Schuhplattler* type. In sober dark clothes, a young farm lad from the great Gudbrandsdal leads out a girl almost as darkly clad as he, the effect brightened by white sleeves and a little discreet embroidery. Like the Swiss pair these two promenade, like the Tyrolese man this young Scandinavian begins his tricks, one eye on his girl. Nothing producing sufficient effect, he mounts her on a chair, gives her a stick to hold, and on its end hangs his hat. This she holds out after the manner of a signboard, while her suitor turns cartwheels on his hands, endeavouring, as he goes over, to kick the hat from off the stick. If he succeeds the couple jaunt round together, if he fails the disgusted lady steps down from the chair and walks away. So much for the celebrated *Halling* of Norway.

Southern Europe produces no such rôles for the men. In the widespread *Saltarello* of Italy the woman plays an equal part with the man; in the famous, though in reality unconvincing *Tarantella,* the two bear the burden about equally. This last

HUNGARIAN CZARDAS

AND A COUNTRY DANCE

appears so different according to the circumstances in which it is done, that it scarcely seems the same dance. Sometimes single persons get up and spin alone until a partner joins them, sometimes several couples stand up together, when they look like a Country dance set, though each pair is in reality dancing together, and a pair formation is, I take it, the normal condition of the spider-named *Tarantella*.

Over the greater part of Spain and Portugal one famous dance for couples holds sway. This is the *Jota* or *Fandango,* which reaches under one name or the other from Valencia on the Mediterranean, to Galicia on the Atlantic. A Spaniard would assuredly question this geographical attribution; a Spaniard from Aragon would flatly contradict it. '*La Jota Aragonesa,*' he would cry, adding to himself (if he managed to keep it to himself), 'Nobody like us!'

Yet even the Aragonese acknowledge a foreign birthplace for their great possession, themselves singing a *Jota copla,* or verse, about its arrival from the south.

From the banks of the Turia
to the banks of the Jalón,
Singing the Jota came
the exiled Aben-Jot.

The music of these *coplas* bears every indication of Andalusian origin, which might mean a Moorish one. So perhaps they are right so far, but to claim the dance as a monopoly of their sun-dried, ochre-coloured Aragon is a slip on their part, for I myself have danced it in Cantabria, Navarre, in the Spanish Basque provinces, and under the name of *Fandango* in French Basque villages as well. And, be it whispered so that Aragon may not hear, I find it more to my taste in the first and the last than in its supposed home. There its glory is enhanced by guitars, and singers with their heads tied up in brilliant silk handkerchiefs, who sing a verse, the guitars giving a stereotyped interlude, after which a couple stands up to dance. Thus they continue, a verse of song and a verse of dance, the dancers moving diagonally across one another, or valsing round a small circle, arms above heads, clacking castanets in triple measure.

A stage *Jota* is springy, lively, showy, but my dance with an Aragonese partner from a village near Huesca disappointed me greatly. Much more enjoyable was a *Fandango* in a French Basque inn, when the accordionist, coming from the Spanish side of the frontier, set himself, from patriotism no doubt, to tire out his French relations. He first gave us sixteen repeats, then twenty at least, but I own I lost count after a quarter of an hour's spinning. A *Fandango* is composed of four figures; multiply these four by thirty-six, and you see the village oil-dealer and the foreign lady circling that kitchen floor one hundred and forty-four times. But they held out, albeit in a hypnotized state, and saved the honour of the French side of the frontier and of the British Isles.

The *Jota* in far-off Valencia cottages is sometimes used as a funeral dance. This brings it into another category, for in these circumstances it becomes highly ceremonial. A description of a dead child lying on a table, decked in her best dress, roses round her head, tallies almost exactly with the description of a funeral wake in Ireland. The observer thought the child was asleep until he saw the candles and the glass of holy water beside her. The sound of the guitar and the clack of the castanets had drawn him in, and to his surprise he saw a young man in the gala dress of the Valencian peasants leading the dance with a girl partner, the musicians and funeral guests urging them on, singing and clapping their hands. It was not done in wild grief, rather was it done in joy that the child had left a troublesome world, and that in the heavens was *un angelito más*.

CHAPTER III

'THE TWIRL AND THE SWIRL'

Many pretty boys and girls
    will pass this way,
Some can dance and some can sing,
By your consent they shall come in.
(*Mummers' Play*)

WE saw in the last chapter how Hungarian peasants decorate the *Czardas* with all sorts of difficult and showy steps. In all dances, even in the modern ballroom kind, there is a tendency for the skilled performer to display his virtuosity, so that it becomes difficult to say exactly at what point the social or recreational dance, done purely for the performers' pleasure, becomes the spectacular dance designed partly if not wholly to appeal to the onlooker.

The examples which spring most immediately to the mind are the wonderful Russian folk dances. Originally, no doubt, these were not spectacular in character, but they have become so in effect, as is shown by their successful incorporation in the Russian Ballets. Some of them are solo dances, and others for pairs and groups, but all are intended primarily for pleasure and only secondly for display. Most famous of all is the 'Cossack' step, in which the dancer squats with crossed arms and shoots out each leg alternately. Incidentally this step is less exclusively Russian than many people realize, for it may be found not only in adjacent countries such as Poland, but as far afield as Ireland, England and Greece, where I have seen it done by Attic shepherds.

Among other striking Russian dances are the Ukrainian *Zaporoschez* for four men with swords, which has a far more martial character than the western Sword dances which we shall see later in this book; and the Georgian Dagger dance which I often saw at Belgrade, performed by Russian *émigrés*. To a lively balalaika tune a man in the dark blue tunic and fur cap of the Transcaucasian peoples, dances round a circle with crossed arms and a dagger held between his teeth. No words can convey the hypnotic character of this dance, nor the gradually increasing tension which leads up to the climax when, his arms still crossed, the dancer with a savage jerk of the head projects the dagger from his mouth, so that it describes a shining parabola through the air and sticks quivering in the floor.

The only dance I have seen to equal this for sheer

dramatic power is the *Dirk Dance* of the Kings of Man, of which Billy Cain has made himself the chief exponent since he was a small boy. Holding the dirk with both hands before him, his eyes fixed on it with the intensity of devotion, the dancer circles round with a light, springing step. Presently he lays it on the ground and continues to dance round and over it, till the climax is reached with a series of lunging obeisances to the dirk. One feels oneself in the presence of something infinitely remote, the dedication perhaps of the weapon which is to serve for some ritual slaying.

In Man we are on the fringes of the Celtic world where the dance, step-dancing mostly, has taken on an obviously spectacular character. Devonshire and Lancashire step-dances (where there is still a dash of the Celt) are sometimes done on a cart that all may see and admire. Irish step-dancing sometimes demands partners, and sometimes a set of dancers as in a Country dance; Highland dancing, though it also needs partners and sets of four, has in it an inherent spectacular quality, and clearly some meaning beyond just the fun of dancing. The Fling is done on one small spot which was once a shield laid flat on the ground, and this brings it into line with dances performed in front of, or over arms, such as the one we have just seen in Man. *Seann Triubhas*, the old trews, once was mimed as well as danced, and seems from the name to have had a comic intention. Anything of the sort has entirely vanished now, and to see a dancer stepping round in lonely circles, kilts swinging, toes pointed, one would think it had never been more than a dancing master's exhibition.

The misty Hebrides have kept alive until just lately (and perhaps the present tense may still tentatively be used) a more mysterious thing. Before the dance a ritual had to be performed on the special day, which was that of St. Michael, September 29th. Crofters circuited the burial-ground of St. Michael on horseback, sun-wise. They made a cake of every sort of grain grown on the farms—a strong magic this—cut it with a special knife, and went out to games and horse-racing. At the evening entertainment the *Cailleach an Dudain* was performed, the *Old Wife of the Mill Dust*. A couple stand up *vis-à-vis*, the man holding a 'magic' willow wand. They circle and change places, he waving the wand over their heads. When the woman feels its touch she falls to the ground. He mimes his grief, bemoans his 'old wife', lifts her left hand, breathes upon it and touches it with the wand, whereupon the dead hand moves slowly up and down. The same magic is applied to the other hand and to the feet. Then kneeling he breathes into her mouth, the woman is filled anew with vigorous life, springs up, and both dance joyfully.

So mysterious a thing belongs rather to the realm of ritual than to that of simple dance, but for what purpose the ritual is enacted it is difficult to say. Autumn is not a usual time for agricultural rites, nor does an evening party appear the moment for them. It might perhaps be love magic. When it is over they all burst into Strathspeys and Foursome Reels. The better known Eightsome Reel does not belong to the Isles, was indeed so 'reconstituted' that one may almost say it was invented, appearing at the Royal Caledonian Ball in London in 1886. One of the fine sights of Highland dancing is the *Reel o' Tulloch* when done as an exhibition dance by four men, their kilts fanning out, their plaids swinging, the pipes skirling out the strange, wild tune, re-inforced by wilder 'hoochs' in high falsetto from the dancers, as they eddy round in their arming.

It is not quite such a far cry as might be expected from our Scottish Highlands to the Highlands of Poland, home of the Polka and of the dances derived from it, the *Mazur, Oberek* and the *Krakoviak*. Quite as spectacular as the Fling are the dances of the Polish Highlanders from Zakopane in the Tatra, whom I must confess to having seen, not in their native fastnesses, but at the Vienna Folk Dance Festival in 1934. The men wore their effective regional costume, white cloaks of heavy homespun cloth, brightly embroidered and fastened across with coloured ribbons, tight trousers of the same material, broad, studded leather belts and shallow hats of black felt like inverted soup-plates, adorned with cowries and eagle feathers, which lend an almost Red Indian look to the tanned, weather-beaten faces. They carried axes, the emblem of their trade, for most of them were woodcutters. Their band of string instruments struck up an immensely vigorous rhythm, and one of them stepped forward, struck his axe into the ground and apostrophized the band with a queer, almost raucous, snatch of song. Then he chose a partner from the little knot of girls in red embroidered skirts, and the pair broke into the *Góralski* or *Mountain Dance.* Now they were together, swinging in a dizzy circle, now apart, the man leaping into the air, and the girl with one hand on her hip and the other at the back of her head, stepping it so fast that the eye could scarcely follow her flashing feet.

Crossing the Carpathians, and descending into the great plains of central Europe, we find in Hungary a great variety of spectacular dances of a different type from the *Czardas.* The best opportunity is the *String of Pearls,* a theatrical performance given at Budapest every year at the St. Stephen's festivities, and consisting of songs and dances from all over Hungary, performed in every case by the authentic peasants whose traditional heritage they are. It will be difficult to forget the women in their lovely dresses, dancing with bottles balanced on their heads, or doing the *Bridal Dance* with embroidered cushions in their hands. The stick dance of swineherds was the exact equivalent of the Basque crossed-stick dance, the Catalan *Hereu Riera* and others of this well-known type, not forgetting our own *Bacca Pipes Jig*, in which we lay clay pipes instead of sticks upon the ground to dance over. Most impressive of all were the men from Kunszentmiklós, who were dressed in silver-buttoned, dark waistcoats, breeches and top-boots, with jackets slung Hussar fashion over one shoulder. In their *Hat Dance* and *Broomstick Dance* they passed their black hats and broomsticks respectively backwards and forwards under each leg as they stepped, the latter an exact replica of our Cotswold dance of the same name. In their *Turkish Dance* they formed a ring and moved a few steps sideways, now to the right and now to the left, holding themselves stiffly erect, their hands away from their sides with a taut rigidity the like of which you must seek in the Pyrenees, when the famous *Saut Basque* is under way.

At its least ceremonial this, the best known of the much talked of Basque dances, may turn about the kitchen table of an inn. At its most ceremonial it will turn about the stage of a *Pastorale* or of a *Cavalcade*, the first in the Soule province, the second in that of Basse-Navarre. Both these folk plays end with a *Saut Basque*, the men, young and old, flooding up on to the rough planks of the village stage, to form a great ring which slowly swings first to the left, then to the right. The solemn movement is decorated with steps, so similar that to the eyes of a non-dancer they are all alike. In reality they ring the changes on *terre-à-terre* step and hop arrangements, so many to the right, so many to the left, quite dull to watch, inexplicably fascinating to do, and ending with a jump, decorated by an *entrechat*—for those who can manage it. The arms are held as stiffly as any arms you have ever seen, only the legs dance. Faces are solemn, minds fully occupied with counting the beats, and remembering where they are in the thousand repeats of a featureless tune. It does not sound particularly interesting, but the dancers find it so, and a *Saut* is so much considered that it may even be put up to auction. Then the village which pays highest has the honour of dancing it first.

There are about nineteen *Sauts*, each with its proper *Suite* to follow it, and by far the most interesting both choreographically and folklorically is the *Seven Jumps, Zazpi Jausiak*. This is known in the Spanish part of the Basque country as well as in the French provinces. You stand in the usual ring for this, move round slowly waiting for a particular bar of music, on which you jump on the spot as high as you can—and that will be very high indeed in the Basque country. The second time the tune is played that bar is repeated twice and you jump twice. The third time you jump three times, and so on up to seven times. A fine sight it is to see a circle of grave men pacing slowly, then shooting up into the air seven times over, as though they could never stop. Then the jumps lessen each time, until they have worked down again and one single jump ends the performance.

Seven ritual jumps are known in other dances and in other lands. One comes from Holland, with an arrangement of repeating bars exactly like that we have just seen. Another comes from Denmark, each of the jumps performed in a different way; and yet another, the most ceremonial of all, comes from Westphalia in Germany. Here a special oak is visited on Easter day and danced round, the dancers trying hard to land after each jump in seven sacred holes in the ground. Those who manage to do so have at least seven more years to live—and then they go and do it again.

If the rigidity of certain Hungarian dancers took us to the Basque country, their *Bridal Cushion Dance* carries us to Norway, where the *Kyndeldans*, dating from the thirteenth century, used to be performed at weddings, and has happily been revived. The girls bear small hanging flower garlands, and after various Country dance figures they thread their winding way through the men who kneel in pairs, holding aloft the flaming torches which give their name to the dance. It is a beautiful and archaic sight, enhanced by the reds, greens and strong deep blues of Norwegian embroidered costumes, and lightened by the shining of the buttons on the men's suits and the flashing of the girls' white sleeves in the smoky and uncertain light of the torches.

These little Norwegian garlands, obtained with such difficulty for a winter wedding, when snow has been on the ground for three months or more, when the sun has not shown his face for at least six weeks, remind us rather incongruously of another set of garlands far away to the south. They were borne about by youths and maidens on the Cantabrian coast of Spain, where it was not much warmer in stormy March weather than it had been amidst the white landscape of the Scandinavian wedding. These north Spanish garlands are for a wedding also, but they are three times the size, and are covered, in a land of flowers, with paper roses. They form quite imposing triumphal arches, and on entering the village cinema one night we unexpectedly found ourselves parading beneath a couple of them, while a cracked piano nobly brought forth the totally unlooked for strains of *God Save the King*. Much flattered and abashed, we were thus escorted to red chairs as though to a royal box, and there were received by the Mayor. The first couple in this Cantabrian dance bears white arches and are supposed to represent the bridal pair, their attendants bear coloured arches, and all describe Country dance figures, *Moulinets, Casts-off* and so on, ending with a promenade under double arches, each person taking one stick of his partner's arch. This effective performance is known as the *Floral Dance of the Mayos and Mayas,* these names being a regional expression for young men and maidens, and not having any connection with May as one might expect. Neither have these triumphal arches anything to do with the Garland dances so closely connected with the Sword dances, which we shall meet in their own place (see Chapter V). Rather are they marks of honour to be raised over the heads of guests, or as we have seen, for a bridal couple to pass beneath, linking up with such processions as the *Treilles* of Languedoc, where arches covered with greenery are brought out for ceremonious occasions.

Before leaving the wild and lovely Cantabrian land, Biscayan breakers roaring in front, great white peaks rearing their heads landwards, let us see yet another little dance, also connected with marriage. It was once done in earnest, but now even Cantabrian girls are too sophisticated to permit any such thing, and it has become a miming game for amusement in the evening, or when people are stirred up to gaiety at those quasi religious outings called *romerias*. The prettiest of all the pretty girls is chosen as the would-be bride, seated in a chair and given a goblet to hold, while her friends circle round her, fingering their tambourines in agile fashion, singing that they must find a dowry for their *Maya* before she can be well married. They go begging amongst the young men standing by, and returning pour their *quête* into the goblet. But the beautiful young bride thinks little of it.

'This won't do,' she says to herself, and rising, sets off in the queerest, smallest, Chinese-like steps, to add to the amount. Holding her cup above her golden head, she shuffles up and down, pirouettes three times, then off she goes to see what she can do, brings back riches and the husband as well, who stands sheepishly beside her chair while the girl friends sing wise advice as to her choice.

> Don't seek the gentleman with the sword,
> Nor him with the cape,
> He will make love to some one else.
> With the pink in his hat,
> A rose behind his ear,
> Seek the lordly boy who knows how to plough.

This is *La Danza de la Maya de la Copa* and one of the most charming things imaginable.

All the dances we have described in this chapter are spectacular only, as it were, by circumstance. In their essence they are recreational or ceremonial. In one corner of Europe, however, the dance as spectacle survives in a tradition unbroken from the time, two thousand years ago, when the Gaditanae, the women of Cadiz, were renowned. According to the younger Pliny no Roman feast would have been complete without these dancing women, who alone were spared, to the number of three thousand, when all foreigners were expelled from the city of the Caesars. The dancers of Andalusia have been perfecting their steps since metals were known, as Mr. H. M. Tomlinson puts it, and to-day they survive in the *Baile Flamenco.* Each of the principal cities of Andalusia has given its name to a dance, as, for instance, Seville to the *Sevillana,* and it was appropriately enough at Seville that, some years ago, I saw my first display of Andalusian dancing.

I was on my first visit to the city of which Spaniards say, 'He who has not seen Seville has seen no marvel.' Some one told me that the best place to see a *Cuadro Flamenco* was the Café de Novedades. You may look for it in vain to-day. It disappeared some years ago, the flimsy wooden structure burnt down or scrapped to make room for improvements. In 1921 it still stood at the far end of the Calle Sierpes, one of the dozen or so famous streets of

Europe and of these the narrowest. No traffic is allowed over the stone slabs with which it is paved, and towards evening, beneath the shadow of the Giralda tower, it becomes the Corso for the youth and beauty of Seville.

First came a turn of a type by no means peculiar to Spain. The performer was a monstrous woman billed as Paquita Morales, *artista sugestiva.* Artist she was not, but it was no over-statement to call her 'suggestive'. Indeed, her songs and dances went beyond the realm of suggestion into that of the fullest exposition. A performance such as hers has been admirably described by Ralph Bates in *Lean Men*, but it was not for this that I had come, and I breathed a sigh of relief when, in a storm of applause, her turn came to an end and the curtain went up on a *Cuadro Flamenco.*

On the stage six or seven people were seated in a ring. The men were dressed in short jackets and trousers tight to the leg, the women in bright embroidered shawls and skirts with the *mantón de Manila* draped gracefully from their high tortoise-shell combs. Their faces showed in varying degrees the flashing looks and dark olive skin of the gipsy, and their figures the lissom lines of that ancient, errant race. The man in the centre held a guitar, the strings of which he began to pluck with nervous fingers. First he thrummed a few resounding chords.

Then like pearls on a string followed a stream of notes, threading up and down the scale, and coming to rest every now and again on that characteristic Phrygian cadence, which gives such passionate poignancy to the music of southern Spain. Gradually the welter of notes and chords sorted themselves into a rhythm, or rather into a combination of rhythms which appeared to struggle for supremacy within the musical fabric. Tapping on the ground, the guitarist's foot lent additional emphasis to beat and counter-beat. Suddenly he ceased, and there was heard a cry so wild, so primitive that it seemed to carry one back to the farthest limbo of time and space. It was a long-drawn-out cry on the one syllable 'Ay', held until it seemed the singer's breath must give out, and then dissolving into a *pianissimo* shower of twists and twirls like a rocket that has burst in the sky, and falls to earth in a thousand glowing sparks.

'*Olé!*' cried the other gipsies, echoing the traditional exclamation of admiring encouragement, which is said to be a relic of the Moslem invocation of Allah.

The voice was again uplifted, and soaring like a bird the song rose and fell until with a final throaty sob it came to an end, and the chorus of *Olés* broke out once more.

Now the guitarist thrummed out a new rhythm,

simpler than the last, but if anything more insistent, more irresistible. The dry clacking of castanets was heard. One of the men strolled lazily towards the middle of the stage and struck an attitude, poised, expectant. Then as though he had received an unseen message, a quiver ran through his body, and his feet, scarcely lifted from the ground, began to stamp out a syncopated counter-point of the music. Head and torso remained immobile and erect, but every now and again his eyes fell on his feet, as though in astonishment that they should be moving to a will other than his own. His arms, too, seemed to be endowed with a life other than his. With sinuous grace they rose and fell, and ever the nimble fingers kept up a ceaseless drumming on the castanets. Louder and more vigorous grew his stamping, tenser and more arrogant his pose, until with head thrown back and an ejaculated *Olé* he struck a final challenging posture. When, later, I saw Massine dance the *Miller's Dance* of his own choreography in the *Three Cornered Hat,* I recalled this moment, and wondered at the perfection with which he had recaptured the spirit of the *Farruca,* and elaborated it according to the principles of his art.

The next dancer was a woman. I learnt afterwards that her name was Maria del Albaicín, but at the time I could not take my eyes off her, even to glance at the programme. Tall and perfectly built, she had that strange beauty, languorous yet vitally tense, which you will only find in a true-bred *gitana*, and in one of a thousand of these. I cannot remember what she wore, only that the predominating colour was red, and that she had a red flower in her dusky hair. The steps of her dance—I think it was a *Malagueña*—were similar to the man's, or looked so to the lay eye. But between them lay the difference which lies between man and woman. His had been a display of masculine strength and pride. Hers was instinct with sensuous and seductive languor, velvet on a frame of steel. Her every movement was the product of that perfect timing, that incalculable balance of proportions which lies behind all great art. Where the man had aroused his audience so that they set their teeth and yelled at him, she laid upon them a spell of silence, which was broken only after she had returned to her place.

A *Cuadro Flamenco,* as such a display is called, is sure to strike the ordinary observer, mindful of Spanish history, as Moorish in feeling. But this impression is mainly illusory. On the ancient native tradition three distinct oriental influences have been grafted. One of these is indeed Moorish, but the others are Byzantine and Romany. *Flamenco* song and dance are in fact a blend of Byzantine line,

Moorish rhythm and gipsy mannerisms of performance. When Moorish rule was at its height in Spain a clear distinction was made between the music of Morocco and the 'Andaluz music of the Moors of Granada'.

The term *Flamenco* requires a word of explanation. *Cuadro Flamenco* means literally 'Flemish Picture'. How did so unsuitable a name come to be given to anything so foreign to northern phlegm? The question is easily asked, but less easily answered. A century ago the name came to be applied in Andalusia to the gipsies, and by extension to anything that had their inimitable dash and verve. But this only shifts the problem a stage farther back. Professor Trend has suggested an ingenious connection with the gaudy flamingos which haunt the marshy banks of the Guadalquivir. Another possibility is that the name came from some inn where gipsy singers and dancers gathered, whose sign was 'The Fleming' and whose landlord might have been in Flanders.

There we must be content to leave it. But it is worth mentioning that the term is properly applied only to the later, more showy and degenerate forms of the art. The purest Andalusian song and dance, the *siguiriyas gitanas, soleas* and *soleares,* together with the *polos* and *martinetes* which are derived from them, claim the more distinguished title of *cante hondo*, or 'deep song', so named from the profound emotions which it expresses, according to some, or from the social depths, the submerged tenth who in prison or low tavern are its truest exponents.

CHAPTER IV

'RING-A-RING O' ROSES'

'Baillarem la Farandola.'
(*Catalan Song*)

ALL over Europe, north, south, east and west, there is one dance which is sure to be a general favourite, perhaps because it is the oldest and the simplest of all. This is the Round dance or Chain dance. Sometimes the circle is closed, and you will be reminded of people dancing round a Maypole or a midsummer bonfire. More often the chain is open, and in this form its history goes back not only as far as ancient Greece, but farther, to that mysterious civilization which flourished four or five thousand years ago in the island of Crete. The ancient Greeks considered the Chain dance to have been invented by Theseus who braved the terrors of the Minoan Labyrinth to rescue Ariadne. The turnings and twistings of the labyrinth, they thought, were shown in the windings of the dance, and they may well have been right, although other authors regarded the dance as representing the swerving flight of the crane.

However this may be, no one who has the good fortune to see it danced, as I did, by the maidens of Megara, can doubt that in its beginnings it was a very solemn and serious business. Megara, the parent city of Constantinople, is to-day a little town of square white houses between Athens and Corinth on the shores of the blue Saronic Gulf. The Attic peasants are always ready to break into dance, but the *Trata,* the *Maidens' Round,* is done only once a year on Easter Tuesday. The women gather on a dusty, open space at the edge of the town, where a number of wine booths have been set up for the occasion. Naturally, they are wearing their finest dresses: tight-waisted, long-sleeved jackets of blue, purple or wine-coloured velvet embroidered in gold; dark, pleated skirts of homespun; and brightly coloured silk petticoats. Round their necks are chains hung with their entire dowry, in gold pieces, fifty to a hundred of them, worth a couple of pounds apiece. On their heads are transparent veils of finely spun silk, covering little caps of small silver coins, sewn together in the manner of chain-mail.

Crossing their arms and linking hands as we do in *Auld Lang Syne,* they form into line and begin to dance, chanting their own accompaniment, a

THE MOREŠKA
AT KORČULA

THE TRATA
AT MEGARA

queer little oriental refrain, repeated as long as the dance lasts. The steps are simple. First, bending forward a little, they move slowly to the right. Then, straightening themselves, they take a few paces backwards. That is all there is to the dance, and it sounds very monotonous. But this very monotony makes it effective, so purposeful does it appear, and so gravely do the women, with downcast eyes, play their part, as the chains serpentine among the crowd, meeting, fusing, and then going their way once more. It is hard to believe that the maidens of ancient Greece looked very different when, in silence, to the singing of the youths, they did the Chain dance in honour of Aphrodite.

Although dancing in modern Greece is not usually quite such a solemn business, all the peasant dances of the country are Chain dances and must have had the same origin. If, on Easter Sunday, you walk uninvited into the barracks of the Evzone Guard in Athens, you will be treated to as fine a display of dancing as you could wish. The Evzones, it must be explained, are the famous kilted soldiers of the President's Guard. Their name literally means the 'beautifully belted ones', although not only their broad pistol belts but their whole uniform is strikingly handsome. On Easter Sunday they have a big midday banquet which, in the course of the afternoon, they shake down with the aid of dances from all the different regions from which they are recruited.

Whether from Epirus, Aetolia, Crete or the Morea, all these dances have a strong family likeness, and it is simplest to divide them, according to their rhythm, into the *Syrtos* or *Kalamatianos* (7/8 time), the *Tsamikos* (3/4 time) and the *Chasapikos* (2/4 time). There is always a fairly simple basic step which is done by all the dancers in the chain (who are linked by handkerchiefs) with the exception of those at either end. These, especially the leader, exhibit the most dazzling display of virtuoso steps which it is possible to imagine. They are governed by no fixed rules. They are the product of an inspiration which none but a native of the country could ever hope to emulate.

The enterprising foreigner, however, can always join in, provided that he is content to stay modestly in the middle of the chain and keep to the basic step. Many is the time that I have danced the *Syrtos* and the *Tsamikos* with grey-smocked shepherds on the slopes of Mount Parnassus, with dwellers (literally and not metaphorically) on the banks of the Styx, and, most frequently of all, with the Evzones themselves.

It was at Megara, watching the maidens, that I met my first Evzone. He made a good beginning by offering me a drink which was particularly welcome in the clouds of dust stirred up by dancing feet. That afternoon I made my first rather inglorious attempts to learn the *Syrtos,* and in the months which followed I often saw my 'beautifully belted' friend again.

In a little Athenian side-street there lies hidden from sight a small underground café patronized by soldiers, boot-blacks and taxi-drivers. It is called the *Elatos,* or, as we should say, 'At the Sign of the Fir Tree'. Here alone in Greece's capital can you see the Greek dances, as opposed to the φοξ τροτ, μπλακ-μποτομ and ρουμπα [1] performed in smarter places of amusement. Here we used to meet Ilias Andoni and his friends Sergent Aristotle, Corporal Socrates and others whose names had an equally familiar ring. The band consisted of a fiddle, a pot-bellied mandolin of exotic appearance, and, played by the inevitable gipsy, the no less inevitable zither. The correct procedure, having ordered drinks, was to drain your glass, hand ten drachmas (say sixpence) to the band, and, having thus paid the piper, to call your tune. You then formed your chain (there was never room for more than one) and began to dance.

I have seen feats of virtuosity at the *Elatos* which would make a man's fortune on the halls, if not in the Russian Ballet. One heavily built N.C.O. from Missolonghi (where Byron 'died that Greece might

[1] Foxtrot, Black Bottom and Rumba.

still be free') used, while dancing, to bend over backwards, until his head touched the floor, and the handkerchief which linked him to his neighbour threatened to tear under the strain. Then with his hair full of sawdust, he would leap to his feet again. Another specialized in the feat of swallowing a pint of beer (Greek beer Ζῦθος brewed, I believe, from onions) from a mug held by his lips alone, while both his thumbs clicked in the air like castanets and he spun round and round on his feet, or bounded into the air. Always while they danced the Evzones had a curious trick of hissing through their teeth. These, strange as it may seem, were the dances to which Byron gave the name of 'dull, Romaic round'.

Evenings at the *Elatos* were interspersed with parties at the house of one of my friends who had a flat high up on the slopes of Mount Lykabettos. Here, during the warm summer nights, on a flat roof that looked far out over the Gulf to the isles of Greece, we had greater space and leisure to learn the dances and also the songs to which, when there is no instrumentalist, they are done. In the basic steps we became fairly proficient, and we even reached the point where, with no critical eyes upon us other than those of our tutors, we ventured to lead and to try a few spinning steps outside the chain, or high leaps, slapping the ground or our own heels in the approved fashion. We would always finish up with the energetic *Chasapikos* which became faster and faster, until worn out we could dance no more.

The *Chasapikos*, with its gay, lilting 2/4 rhythm, might almost be a Serbian *Kolo*, and the words to which we used to sing it hint at such a connection:

> The young Serbian girls, they call them little, green quinces;
> Little, green quinces, that's what they call the girls.

The Chain dance is indeed the characteristic dance of all south-eastern Europe. It is called *Kolo* in Yugoslavia, *Horo* in Bulgaria, and *Hora* in Roumania, all slightly varying forms of the Greek word *choros*, the generic name for the dance. To the lay eye there is no very great difference between the dances of these three countries, and at the Folk Dance Festival at Vienna seeing Roumanians and Bulgarians in leather jackets and loose skirted trousers of white linen, do their *Sărba Jancului*, their *Ca la Breaza* from the Prahova Mountains, and their *Ratchenitza* to the electrifying fiddling of gipsy musicians I was vividly carried back to the years I spent in Yugoslavia. In the Balkans, dancing seems to be associated with all the pleasantest memories of travel, for dancing is an essential part of the people's lives. It is not merely an amusement; it is recreation, exercise, self-expression, intoxication, a pursuit to be indulged in on the great festive occasions of wedding or *slava* (family saint's day) and no less during an hour's wait between trains at a wayside station.

There are innumerable different *Kolos*, some grave and others lively, some in 2/4 time, others in 3/4, some done with small, quick, intricate steps and your arms round your neighbours' neck, others, like the *Arapsko Kokonjeste*, done hand-in-hand with great sideways leaps, the circle now narrowing and now dramatically opening to its fullest extent as the leader cries, '*Otvori!*'

With the *Kolo* is linked one of my most unforgettable memories of Belgrade. It was in 1925, the evening of the Court Ball at the Old Palace in King Milan Street. In the vast white and gilt ballroom the guests awaited King Alexander and Queen Marie. Nine years later that very room was to be transformed into a *chapelle ardente* for the murdered King. But no shadow of approaching tragedy hung over the throng of beautiful women and men in brilliant uniforms. The band struck up the King's *Kolo*, the doors were flung open, and the Royal pair appeared, not striding in majesty, but leading a long, winding chain of diplomats and Court officials in the simple steps of the Chain dance.

In Serbia, early spring is the season of weddings, and if you want to see dancing here is your chance. They last three days with the religious ceremony on the second. During these three days feasting and dancing never cease. From the moment when, in her elaborate wedding-costume, the bride is presented to the company, she is not allowed, even on the night after the ceremony, to stop waiting on the guests and dancing with any who do her the honour of inviting her.

I had a peasant friend called Jovan Joksimović who asked me to be the *stari svat* at his wedding. The functions of a *stari svat* may be described as those, not of a best man (the *kum* is that) but of a sort of 'second-best man'. He has to see (and drink) the whole thing through from start to finish. Fortunately perhaps I left the country before Jovan had saved enough to get married. I should certainly have had to take a week's leave for the event, three days for the wedding and another three to recover from it.

It would be tedious to describe the countless variations of the Chain dance in the different countries of Europe. Suffice it to say that it is popular in central Europe, especially in Germany where the *Reigen* have taken a new lease of life since National Socialism has promoted a return to old German song and dance. These *Reigen* date back to the days of the old Minnesinger in the early Middle Ages. In baronial castles the dance chain used to be formed in the dining-hall after the midday meal. Men and women joined alternately in the chain which would move round to the left (sun-wise, that is to say) with slow, gliding steps to the singing of the leader. The other dancers would take up the refrain in chorus. Sometimes the leader carried a beaker of wine in his hand, or, anticipating my Evzone, would dance with it balanced on his head. These dances, called *Tanz* when slow and stately or *Reigen* when more lively, corresponded respectively with the French *Carole* and *Espringale* or *Tresque*, Chain dances done by Lords and Ladies in the days of the Troubadours. The name *Carole* had, according to Gaston Paris, the special meaning of 'dancing a round dance accompanying oneself with song'. It is probably derived from the same Greek root as the word *choros*, and is, of course, the origin of our own sung 'carols', as we have already seen.

In later medieval times the name given to the French Round dance was *Branle*, a name which still survives not only in the country districts of France, but as far afield as Roumania where the *Braul* is a favourite and very lively *Hora*. In his *Orchesographie* Thoinot Arbeau gives the steps of the *Branle* as danced in the sixteenth century, together with the tune which will be familiar to many from Peter Warlock's fascinating *Capriol*. We should describe these steps to-day as two *chassés* to the left followed by one to the right, and in this very form it still survives in the ballad dances of the Faeroe Islands, to which the Chain dance came probably by way of England and Scandinavia. These ballad dances are done at the Feast of St. John and at the National Festival (July 29th). They are accompanied in the best traditional style by the singing of old ballads and folk songs. The chain, closed at first, is later opened by the leader, and in its labyrinthine windings the dance resembles the end of the *Lancers* at a rowdy house-party.

In France the Round dance kept its aristocratic character through the days when the *Roi Soleil,* Louis XIV, himself *menait le Branle,* and there is a story of Lully, the great Court musician, seated on a kitchen table playing a *Branle,* while the palace servants danced.

But it had its sinister side, too, for by all accounts this was the principal dance done by the witches at their Sabbaths. It is generally accepted to-day that witchcraft, on account of which so many people were brought to trial in the fifteenth, sixteenth and seventeenth centuries, was no figment of the superstitious imagination, but the very real practice of a pre-Christian fertility cult which persecution had driven underground, but which survived nevertheless, and perhaps is still alive. Of this cult the Round dance was one of the most important ceremonies, done round the 'Devil' (who was the priest of the cult) or led by him. In the English witch trials it is mentioned but not described. It is in Scotland, in Sweden and in France that we hear of it in greatest detail. A peculiarity seems to have been that the dancers faced the outside not the inside of the ring, and, as they moved always to the left, were always going widdershins, against the sun. 'Et à certaine cadence ils se choquent et frappent impudiquement cul contre cul,' concludes De Lancre, that staid Counsellor from Bordeaux, who was sent south at the beginning of the seventeenth century to extirpate witchcraft in the French Basque province of Labourd.

A yet darker rôle was played by the Chain dance in the French Revolution, when the *gensses dou Midi* took their dance to Paris and used it for propaganda purposes. Immensely long chains tore through the streets, wound round the trees of Liberty, as in happier times they wound round traditional trees in the villages of the South, catching up passers-by, magistrates, generals, to the tune which then became the *Carmagnole*. Next, with the inconsistency of the mob spirit, it was used in defence of those very Bourbon Kings which it had mocked. In 1815 the Bonapartists of the Midi fled before it, for once taken in its coils they would be thrown down and trodden beneath a hundred dancing feet. In the streets of Toulon a Bonapartist leader, General

Ramel, was caught by a *Farandole* and killed to the shouts of '*Vive le Roi*'.

To-day the *Farandole* is still preserved in Provence, kept alive by Sociétés de Farandoleurs with picturesque names such as 'Les Libellules Arlésiens', 'Les Joyeux Mineurs' or 'Les Hirondelles'. You may see it done on special occasions such as the festival of *La Bravade* round the midsummer bonfires at Aix, that of *La Tarasque* at Tarascon, or more simply at a bull-fight.

We are in the huge arena of Nîmes. Here, where wild beasts once fought men, men now fight bulls. They are raking the lifeblood of the last victim out of the sand when into the ring comes a long thin line of dancers. It circles sun-wise round the arena to the sound of the Provençal pipe and the continuous beat of the Provençal drum. It is led by a boy of eighteen or so, who holds the hand of a girl of his own age. She holds the hand of a sixteen-year-old, who in turn grasps that of a smaller child. The line dwindles down to two infants of five and four who painstakingly bring up the rear. The boys are dressed in white with violet waist sashes and big violet bérets, the girls in smart white frocks, violet ribbons and the highest of high heels.

The file works its way round sideways, a step to the left, then another, a slight hop on the right foot together with a *grand battement* with the left leg.

The *grand battement* takes an exceedingly pointed toe almost to waist level, and the painstaking infants at the tail stagger. The gay, cheap air which should at least cover its cheapness by rhythm and exhilarating speed decorously follows the cramped paces of the dancers. Now the step changes: *cabrioles* follow, little shuffling *pas de Bourrée, entrechats,* steps of the modern ballet, poorly executed and fitted poorly to the music. Finally, saved up to the end, the boys give the Kibby or Cossack step, squatting on their haunches, kicking out each leg in turn until the infants at the end sit abruptly on the sand.

Having completely held up all forward movement, the file may wait still a little longer. Out comes the best boy, the prize pupil, to execute his solo known as *Cavalier Seul.* Before the line can get into motion again and make its seemly exit, a figure leaps the barrier. Another follows and another. The dignified people in the expensive shady seats sit tranquilly in their places, but the more impatient *soleil* scale the barrier, drop on the sand like bees dropping from a swarm, invade the arena, swallowing up the decorous *Enfants du Midi,* and somehow sort themselves into single file. Now for a moment we may see what a *Farandole* must have been before the *maîtres de danse* laid hands upon it, what it still may be on a wedding night or after a village feast. These men pull upon each other's arms, they put their weight, they put speed, they put a taste of life and energy and wine and sun into it.

We turn southwards into the treeless, sun-smitten country of vineyards. The red ochre coast runs down into Spain, the great white Canigou looks over French Catalonia to an ultramarine sea. When the sturdy Catalans are full of red Banyuls they can dance a *Farandole* as well as any one.

Here they come, round the Square of a village in the valley of the Tet, the leader in a scarlet *barretina* like a Phrygian cap, the elder women in caps of fine white lace stretched over a black silk lining. The men have their arms round their partners' waists, and they just walk quietly and jauntily in time to the music, in couples round a wide circle. The leader and his lady raise a scarlet arch—it is the man's waist-sash—and beneath it run all the couples. Then comes *L'Escargot*: the leading man turns his lady under the sash, the rest sort themselves into a single file and all, holding hands, follow the first lady. Now the leader is off again, taking his followers through the streets, round trees, into inns and out again, till back on the Square they break into couples as at the beginning. Now is the great moment for the men. Holding their partners by the inside hand, turning towards them, they show off their most varied steps, *brisés, pas battus* and whatnot. At the next change of music they end with a frenzied gallop round the Square, then, as though shamed of a sudden into sobriety, walk away demurely to the plaintive little final tune.

At some time or other—before Cervantes wrote his *Ilustre Fregona* in which he mentions it—a religious revival must have seized upon the ancient care-free Chain dance on the coast of Spanish Catalonia. A doleful *Divino* took the place of what must have been a gay, probably Bacchic song, and for long years the *Contrapás* swung to and fro devoutly outside church doors, led by the priests, waiting for night and *fiestas* to turn it into the *Farandole* again. One set of men's voices proclaims that they are all miserable sinners. Another set answers that indeed they are and will all be justly punished, and the line is pulled to the left by the *Cap*, to the right by the *Cua*. The *Contrapás* is dying out once more to-day, though the little town of Olot still favours it occasionally.

A quite modern outcome of the *Contrapás*, and so of the Chain from which it was born, is the famous *Sardana*, supposed to have been invented by old Pep Ventura, the musician, which I take leave to doubt, for no one person ever yet invented a folk dance. It has become the symbol of Catalan liberty, and no political gathering is complete without its *Sardanas*. At the sound of the insistent 2/4 rhythm people fly together like needles to a magnet. In one moment the great ring is formed, in another it is under way, monotonous, hypnotic, deadly to watch, wonderful to do. The real place to see it is at Barcelona at a *Sardana Aplec* (gathering) in the park, when toughs from the dockside streets, students from the University, little midinettes and large lady duennas, each wearing the intent *Sardana* face, swing and sway with one accord for hours together. They seem to find in it some national energizer, though to a non-Catalan it looks like soothing syrup.

All along the Pyrenees we may follow the twistings of the Chain dance, winding up into mountain valleys and out again into the poplar-fringed meadows of the plain. It is the *Galop Infernal* of Aude, the *Branlou Bach* or *Low Branle* of Béarn, the *Ronde Ouverte* and *Courrento* of Gascony and *La Pamperruque* of Bayonne, this last done before the Dauphin himself in 1781, the dancers linked with garlands instead of handkerchiefs, the first and last gentlemen carrying beribboned wands.

Now we are on the edge of the Basque country, that richest of all repositories of old, forgotten things. On the French side of the Pyrenees *Karrika Dantza*, the Street dance, and *Soka Dantza*, the String dance, are both *Farandoles*, but it is left to the Spanish side to give to the *Aurresku* a character more solemn and more ceremonial than the Chain dance has kept anywhere else in Europe.

A fine summer Sunday afternoon, an afternoon made for dancing, brings every one out on to the plaza of the village. The plaza slopes down the mountain-side towards the grey-blue waters of the Bay of Biscay. It is shaded by plane trees, and the *Ayuntamiento,* the Mayor and Corporation, sit on a bench beneath them. The Corporation have their own band consisting of a single pipe-and-tabor. With his left hand the *Txistulari* holds the three-holed pipe to his mouth; with his right he beats the little drum hanging from a strap round his neck. Sailors have strolled up from the harbour, fresh from their poaching in French waters; young farmers have come down from the heights, and there are girls in the newest fashions from San Sebastian, with beautifully waved hair, each with her small mantilla of black lace over her arm, just come out of Vespers. The men are in white, scarlet waist-sashes showing off their lithe Basque figures, scarlet or blue bérets on their heads.

Now a long string of young men forms behind the best dancer, the *Aurresku* or First Hand, who gives his name to the dance. Taking the man behind him with his left hand, he leads him round in a wide circle and comes to a standstill before the bench where the Mayor sits in state and in judgement. Snatching off his béret, the *Aurresku* bursts into showers of wonderful steps. Out comes the last man in the line, the *Atzesku* or Last Hand. He dances, the leader replies. They wear set faces, for this is a challenge, a duel in dance. Suddenly the piping stops, and there is an awesome roll on the drum. An arch is made by the *Aurresku* and his neighbour, and the file passes beneath it. 'Here comes a chopper to chop off your head', as in *Oranges and Lemons,* and the opportunity is taken to weed out unruly spirits or those who have been too long in the tavern.

Now comes the solemn part of the ceremony. The *Aurresku* sends four of his men to beg his chosen lady to honour him. Out they march, and compel a seemingly indifferent, even unwilling, damsel to accompany them. She is led to the place of honour and there stands prisoner, two men on either side, the *Aurresku* exactly *vis-à-vis*. Off comes his béret again, and he breaks out into a display of steps different and even more wonderful than the first. He leaps violently three feet off the ground, throwing up each foot alternately until it nearly hits him in the face. Then he pauses and moves so gently now that you think you were mistaken and that he never leapt at all. You think of the bower bird posturing before his mate, but soon the hunched shoulders, the streaming brow, the glazed eyes destroy so pretty a comparison, and you become conscious of the animal brutality of the performance. He takes on the appearance of a Minotaur, a bull dancing, if so monstrous a fantasy can be imagined, before his female. And all this to a charming and delicate little tune on the pipe.

After several of these curious little pauses, during which the performing male seems to consider how next to display his prowess, the *Aurresku* finishes with a final bravura and three polite bows, to the left, to the right and to his patient lady. Then, the perspiration pouring down his face, he presents her with one end of a handkerchief, himself holds the other end and leads her into the circle. It is a century since the Church, straining at a gnat while swallowing the camel, introduced the modestly separating handkerchief. The *Atzesku* sends for his partner and establishes his right to her with the same Bird of Paradise display, and so should they all, right into the houses if the girl is shy. But modern impatience cuts short the ceremonial, and the rest seek their partners in a body. The line, what with handkerchiefs and girls, is now trebled in length. Another bridge is made, the music changes to a *Fandango,* the string breaks into couples, and we leave them hard at it, scattered all over the plaza.

On one day in the year an even more ceremonial *Aurresku* is danced in the principal square of San Sebastian. It is the opening day of the annual

Semana Vasca or Basque Week. The young President, Don Antonio de Orueta, a dancer of no mean powers, sends his four men into the *Casa Consistorial,* the Town Hall, to fetch the Mayoress. Then in top hat and frock-coat he dances before her. It is a wonderful sight, this ceremonial opening in the great *Plaza de la Constitución,* beneath rows of balconies still bearing their numbers from the days when this was the bull-ring and the balconies the boxes. Stranger, and in a way still more wonderful, was the opening *Aurresku* at the *Conferencia de Estudios Vascos* (Conference of Basque Studies) at Vergara in July 1930, when top-hatted and béreted delegates from all the provinces joined with bearded scholars from foreign lands and from Basque colonies over the seas, in this manifestation of ancient traditions.

To the west, at the farthest limits of the Old World, the Cantabrian Mountains slope down to the green, undulating hills of Galicia and Portugal, and the magic circle of the dance dwindles into gay little rounds such as children love: the *jogos de roda* or singing games of the Lusitanian seaboard. These are done on festival days by the stocking-capped fishermen of the Atlantic Coast, the hooded shepherds of the Estrela Mountains or the maidens of the Lima Valley, all decked out in scarlet and gold. To some gay little Portuguese tune the dancers walk round in a ring. Then to a livelier refrain they break into pairs and swing round or jig opposite each other, clapping hands or clicking their fingers like castanets. Such dancing is not far removed from the childish innocence of *Here we go round the Mulberry Bush* and *Ring-a-Ring o' Roses,* and at this point, shorn of its ancient solemnity, we may take leave of the Round dance, once, as Sir James Frazer puts it, 'the most serious occupation of the sage, become at last the idle sport of children'.

CHAPTER V

'THREE MEET'

I

In comes I that's never been before,
Six merry actors stand at your door.
They can merrily dance and sing,
And by your leaf they shall walk in.
(*Mummers' Play*)

THAT is what they are, actors, singers and dancers, and that is why the arm on our sign-post pointing to midwinter scenery was inscribed with a double name, 'Mummers and Sword Dancers'. For although the first incline to drama and the second to dance, it would be unreasonable to separate one from the other. To them must be added the Plough Stots, who sometimes, with swords in hands, dance before the Plough Monday ploughs, and the Soulers and Pace-eggers also, both of whom give their play out of season, the first on All Souls' Day, the last at Easter, as their name (a corruption of Pasch egg) denotes. The proper time for all of them is midwinter. The country of the Plough Stots and the Soulers is Lincolnshire and Cheshire respectively. The geographical distribution of Sword dances, clustering thickest in what was England's Danemark, has encouraged theories of Scandinavian, and more lately of Germanic origin. Any such conclusion is, however, absolutely untenable, as we hope to show, when Slav, Italian, French, Basque, Spanish and Portuguese Sword dances are known and allotted their due position. In this country then, their habitat stretches sporadically from Shetland to Yorkshire, the Mummers' play covering a still larger area of the British Isles, with an example or two from Ireland, the Scottish Lowlands, Wales and the Isle of Man, bunching thickly in the Cotswolds, and reaching as far east as Essex, as far west as Cornwall. Where the play meets the Sword dance it lends its well-worn lines to the dancers, merges and dwindles into a mere song for introducing the performers, yet clings to its essential theme in some such verse as

An actor he is dead,
  And on the ground he's laid.
We'll have to suffer for it,
  Brave boys, I'm sore afraid.

Properly dressed Mummers—too often they consider a black face sufficient disguise—are to my mind one of the best sights left in old England, and of the properly dressed I recommend those of Longparish and Overton in Hampshire. I shall not forget my first visit to these last, nor the finding of them standing in the snow on Christmas Day in the morning, against a background of ancient red brick in the village of Freefolk—a name teeming with Wessex history, and earned before ever St. George or the Turkish Knight walked its street. Their paper streamers lashed about them in the wintry wind, their dragon like the hobby-horse was 'forgot', but they sang a good old carol calling blessings on

> The Master of this house,
> With a gold chain round his neck.

Father Christmas presented each player in ancient words so jumbled by usage and oral transmission that he does not understand them himself. 'King' George killed off his infidel antagonist, the ten pound Doctor, in a high hat wreathed with paper ribbons, brought him to life again, a queer character without *raison d'être*, wearing a bunch of dolls tied to his back, proclaimed himself

> Little Johnny Jack,
> With his wife and family on his back,

and the old leader, whose sons are all in the play,

and who claims three hundred years of family participation, carefully covered his face with his streamers, remarking, 'They mustn't know who I be.'

Although any dancing is now likely to be a *pas seul* by the cleverest member of the company, it seems certain that Mummers did once dance, and probably a Sword dance. I have had the honour just recently, of assisting the resurrection of a Mummers' play thought to be dead these forty years. Yet, after a chance word revealing its existence, it only needed a meeting of some old fellows who remembered, and some not so old who themselves had played, to hear the stereotyped speeches coming from lips which had not recited them for nearly half a century. Their advance description of their costumes—of newspapers, they said—sounded decadent and dull, but having manufactured them themselves from their own recollections, they burst upon the startled village in full array, paper streamers covering their faces, floating from their high, awe-inspiring hats—replicas of the Overton Mummers who have never lapsed and of whom these Marshfield (Glos.) men had never heard. Further, having said they carried sticks, they made themselves wooden swords and with one accord started marching round sun-wise with a springy, dancing step. I expected the Sword dancers' Lock every minute.

It never came, for Mummers produce antagonists and a duel, while Sword dancers do their killing *en masse*, cutting off their Captain's head, or displaying the Lock as a symbol of his death.

The Captain, taking the place of the Mummers' Father Christmas, presents his men in a 'Calling-on Song', each man stepping out under some historical name, Lord Nelson, Napoleon, Collingwood, or under such fancy titles as 'Jerry, the passionate friend', or the less glamorous 'Hickman, a rival'. When all have thus been announced and are marching sedately round a sun-wise circle, they suddenly bring their swords together in a pyramid shape, and clash them in the centre for some eight or sixteen bars of the music, withdraw them, and each man, giving the point of his own sword to the man behind, grasps the point of the sword in front of him, so that they are linked up in the regulation, yet inexplicable hilt-and-point formation, in which Sword dancers march from the Baltic to the Mediterranean. Folk art is seldom brief, and the succession of serpentining figures all looking much alike palls on the spectator after a while, but never on the dancers. The longsword dances show clearer figures, the men being farther apart; the rapper or pliable shortswords bunch their holders tightly together and make it impossible for the audience to follow the pattern. In longsword dances suddenly opening rings come as a relief; in rapper dances the bars of step-dancing break the monotony, as do straight lines wherein the middle man jumps over a sword held some three feet off the ground, followed by his two neighbours who jump together, one on either side of him. The quick break-away of a long Hey, or a Roll, wherein they pass in couples beneath the swords, is spectacular and easier to follow. At these moments the accordions pump out their north-country tunes with greater zest, and those who are lucky enough to have a drummer step it cheerily to a livelier beat. Although the flutter of ribbons and handkerchiefs beloved of Morris men is absent, mirrors flash from caps, rosettes splash colour on clean, white shirts, and it is a good sight on the grey cobblestones of a northern village under a smoky, midwinter sun. The figures are marvellously varied considering that the men are linked together as described above, and that this chain, be it twisted inside out or tied up in knots, never comes undone until it is time to form the culminating Lock. This shining polygon of woven swords is then put round the victim's neck, or rolled along the shoulders of each in turn all round their circle, or held aloft to throw on the ground with a crash. At Askham Richard they lunge into the middle of the ring, sword points inwards, in a really terrifying manner, and the first time I saw them at it I expected, as after a visit from Cruel Lambkin in the Border song, to see 'blood on the floor'. And all the time the Fool runs round them yelping, or giving vent to queer little chirps, and Betsy, a man in draggled skirts, indulges in odds and ends of step-dancing.

Highland Sword dances are better known, or rather what is called *the* Highland Sword dance, *Gilly Callum,* a solo over sword and scabbard crossed on the ground. In reality it is one of three. The others, the Argyllshire and the Lochaber Broad-swords, are for four men, very showy and more ceremonial. Sword dances have no such written history as the Morris, but we do just catch a glimpse of the hilt-and-point type of Sword dance now and then, both in England and Scotland. The Perth Skinners' Company entertained Anne of Denmark with their dance in 1590, when five men stood on the shoulders of five more, a kind of glorified hoisting of the leader, exactly paralleled to-day in an Aragonese village. A Cavalier gentleman, living in Lancashire, mentions a Sword dance in his diary, as given on Ash Wednesday 1638, and quotes the Prologue, written for the occasion, one would say, rich in classical allusions and terrible stuff to get into a country lad's head.

Forget the Muses' Hill, those nymphs, those dames,
And practise with our swords th' Olympic Games. . .

The Cavalier gentleman's grandson inherited the diary habit, and gives us another glimpse in 1712, when he actually composed a Sword dance for a special occasion.

June 3rd.—I made a Sword dance against my marlpit is flowered.

June 7th.—I began to teach the 8 sword dancers their dance which they are to dance at the Flowering of my marlpit.

He was very busy next day making caps for the marlers and dancers, and the eight dancers practised in the barn, and on the great day danced in the marlpit itself, which was 'flowered very much to the satisfaction of ye spectators'. Afterwards they baited a bull in it, and had a Maypole in it also, so when the work of marling (liming) the fields was done it is hard to see.

It has been said that Sword dancers do their necessary killing *en masse,* and to ensure their anonimity they sometimes produce some such line as:

'I'm sure it's none of I
That did this awful crime,'

each throwing the blame on the next man. Nevertheless some dances show both the antagonists' duel of the Mummers' play and a normal Sword dance killing by all the dancers together; some villages possess both a Sword dance and a Mummers' play;

while Ampleforth possesses a long, abnormal play, most of the normal one and two Calling-on Songs, all combined with the Sword dance. But in every dance some one is killed, or the symbol of his death is held aloft; in every play this some one is raised to life again by a comic cure. *They have to.* Which italicized assertion takes us straight to a Basque village up near the Pic d'Orhy, and a stern Basque voice saying above the jingle of the bells and the thud of the springing feet: '*Il faut qu'ils le fassent.*'

'What is the play?' asked a Boxing Day motorist in Marshfield Street, when he pulled up to watch the strange, shaggy figures looming mysteriously out of the hill mist which hung over what was once the march dividing Celt from Saxon.

The play is the oldest play in the world, for it depicts the death of the Old Year, of winter, of scarcity; it brings in the New Year, the hope of spring, plenty. It is sympathetic magic of the most essential sort, for you kill to make sure old, worn-out things are killed, you bring alive again to ensure the Renewal with its abundance. What you do Nature will do also. To make this fearsome task a little lighter some one must personify the giver of warmth and life, and that some one would naturally be the Chief, the Great Man among the people, for never must his powers be impaired or with his failing strength all life would fail. He must then die in his vigour, and one younger and still more vigorous must replace him. If the Great Man cannot be spared then some other must take his place, or at least a mimic death must be enacted at the time of the Year's death. Thus baldly must the now well understood principle of the Dying God be sketched, and those who have not read this fundamental subject may be referred to special studies, notably to those of Mexican Corn gods, and, of course, to Frazer's masterly work, *The Golden Bough*.

Mixed up with this winter solstice rite are certainly rags and tatters from other ancient doings of mankind. Agricultural rites with their ploughs and ears of corn attached themselves very early, besides a medley of later doings picked up on a journey down the ages. It is folly to acknowledge one origin alone in a rite which appears to have come into Europe with, at least, the Indo-European peoples. Nevertheless nothing but a seasonal necessity explains the inalienable attachment to the winter solstice. Sword dancers do not know what they are doing, of course; they are just 'carrying on', and Mummers are but reciting ridiculously corrupted lines drawn from an Elizabethan St. George play. But everything is built on something else, and below St. George is a foundation so deeply dug by every European race that it is impossible to assign it to any particular diggers. Ancient Rome already had trouble over folk foundations, in spite of centuries of State religion and Olympic divinities, while the casting of the blame on some one else takes our thoughts beyond Rome to older Athens, where after the annual killing of the sacred bull the killers ran away, throwing the blame of the 'Ox-murder' on the axe which did the deed. So fathoms below St. George and the Turkish Knight we find that ubiquitous man in woman's clothes, our northern Betsy, sometimes hugging a bastard baby, sometimes masquerading as a bride, and a skin-clad being, jingling with bells, comic yet looked at askance, and a second man, the hairy Fool's projection perhaps, lording it over the rest, yet born to be killed at the turn of the year. Small wonder the Marshfield motorist asked: 'What is the play?'

II

> The bagpipe and the Morris bells
> That they are not far hence us tells.

The third arm of our signpost pointed to Whitsuntide and May, and, as you will remember, was marked with one word only, *Morris*. We will now follow that green lane and come appropriately to

Bampton-in-the-Bush, as I did one Whit Monday morning. The broad street was quiet and empty, but wandering on disappointedly, a faint fiddling came to my ears, a farm gate swung open, and out on to the road danced the Morris men of Bampton. They wore their clean 'whites', bell-pads on their legs, ribbons on their chests and arms, billycock hats on their heads dressed up like Maypoles with early roses, peonies and green leaves. They were moving off from the farm in their processional dance, *Green Garters,* accompanied by flourishing white handkerchiefs and a gay fiddle tune. Down the road they came, to stop outside an inn where the procession gave place to a stationary dance, *The Gallant Hussar,* its figures engagingly named Foot-up, Gip, Back-to-back, Heys and Half-Rounds. After that a very old man gave a solo Morris jig to the tune of *Princess Royal,* to which the song called *The Arethusa* was once written. His hand movements were as quietly elegant as those of a ballerina; his aged features wore a self-satisfied expression, for he had lived for this moment since last Whit Monday. Off they went again, and this time *Green Garters* took them into the Rectory garden, where particularly hard dancing and a hearty meal dissipated the effects of the numberless morning drinks. Little girls hung on the outskirts of the dance, bearing Mayhoops between two of them, two wooden hoops garlanded

THE BAMPTON (OXFORDSHIRE) MORRIS MEN (*above*)
THE OVERTON MUMMERS (*below*)

with greenery, and thrust one inside the other at right angles. The Cake and Sword Bearer made an impressive figure, the first impaled on the point of the second and only to be cut for those who paid. A slice was then carried away to be placed under the buyer's pillow, and slept on 'for luck'.

About a year afterwards I stood in the streets of a Basque town when shrill music came to my ears, and insistent, fiery drumming. A door in a wall burst open and out came a procession of white-clad dancers, bells ringing, ribbons flying, little sticks clashing, a Fool in a tall, pointed cap following, a masculine 'Lady' in Basque shawl and stiff starched petticoats, elegantly parading. These Morris men, of the most distant of all European stock from their Bampton fellow artists, danced in single file, string soled *espadrilles* greatly improving their lightness, but their figures were much the same, Rounds and stick-tapping with their opposite numbers; their very step was our Morris step, their very tune our *We won't go Home till Morning*. This was my first lesson in comparative study, and I gasped.

The Bampton Fool and Fiddler have been rolled into one nowadays, but in the great days of Morris the former was distinct enough, as the Squire, or Rodney, wearing a fox-skin, its tail hanging down his back, carrying a cow-tail with which he lashed his men and the lookers-on.

'Six Fools and one Morris dancer!' is his well-worn joke as he fiddles away, dancing about a little to the beat of *Bobbing Joe* and *Glorishears*, one leg clad in yellow, the other in white.

Bampton has lost another character also, and that a most important one, since she is found all over Europe. No man-woman now accompanies the dancers, and it must be acknowledged she is not missed, for in spite of her ubiquity she never appears to have very much to do. She called herself Maid Marian in the Morris country, and from a primitive character of the Sword dancers' Betsy type, polished herself into some semblance of the improbable lady member of Robin Hood's company, and with her new name was taken to belong to the Sherwood foresters rather than to her real companions, the Morris. She is seen in two early pictures of the Morris, where the Sherwood men do not appear, and Laneham's often quoted letter from Kenilworth about 1575 shows her in what was probably her proper place, Robin Hood again conspicuously absent. 'A lively Morris dance,' he writes, 'according to *the ancient manner,* six dauncerz, Mawd-Marion and the fool.'

Again when Henry VIII took his Queen a-maying in Greenwich Park and Robin Hood and his men met them with fancy shooting, Maid Marian did not put in an appearance—but neither did the Morris.

She did not maintain her new elegance for very long it seems, but, reverting to the Betsy manner, indulging in the grotesque antics apparently inseparable from men in petticoats, fell into disrepute and disrepair, and called down upon herself such remarks as, 'The May Marrians were men in women's clothes contrary to Deut. xxii. 5'—and this from no Puritan.

Bampton has lost its Hobby-horse, too, although he was well known in the district, so, exciting as their dancing day still is to us, it would appear dull and incomplete to Tudor eyes, when all middle England heard the jingle of the bells, the shrilling of the three-holed pipes, the thundering of the drums and the prancing of the Hobby-horse from May Day till midsummer.

At one time they were so highly considered that dresses, bells and musicians were provided from parish funds, so that from Church-wardens' and civic accounts we can follow their progress in popularity. Four items of this sort may be given:

1509	Silver paper for the Mors daunsers.	11d
	For VI peyre of shone for ye Mors daunsers.	4s
1529	For Fyve ells of canvas for a Cote for Made Maryon.	XVIId
1557	Payed to the Minstrells and the hobby horse uppon May Day.	3s.

To help a lively picture of them we have their portraits painted on glass in the celebrated Betley window, which although now found to date only from the seventeenth century, most certainly copied fifteenth-century figures. It appears as though they had been adapted by a rustic and more sober hand from the extravagant personages of Israel van Mechlen's Flemish engraving on copper of about 1470, every Betley dancer finding his prototype here in dress and pose, Friar Tuck and the Maypole obviously added to suit English taste.

But presently approbation, though not popularity wanes; the jingling company draws upon itself first disapproval, then absolute hatred from the Puritanical-minded. It is thanks to these horror-stricken gentlemen that we have further and still more lively pictures of the Morris, such as this:

'Then march the heathen company towards the church, their pypers playing, their drummers thundering, their stumps dancing, their bells jingling, their handkerchiefs fluttering about their heads like madde men, dancing and swinging their handkerchiefs over their heads in the Church like devils incarnate.'

Thus writes one in 1583. invoking so exciting a vision that it is certain, quite contrary to his intention, every one ran out to look next time they heard the clamour of the bells. His diatribe had no effect, however, for thirty years later we find amongst many others, one Richard Mee excommunicated for absenting himself from divine service, and 'being in company with Morris dancers since Whitsundaye laste paste', and even the musician suffered for 'pypinge at the same', while another thirty years later one of the questions put to Churchwardens in the Archdeaconry of York was:

'Whether hath your Church or Churchyard been prophaned by . . . Lords of Misrule, Summer Lords, Morris Dancers?'

Yet in spite of the disrepute into which the old ceremony fell, so popular did it remain with the common folk that the name presently passed into current English, so that a writer, hitting the nail on the head more accurately than he knew, likens them in 1621 to 'the Salii in the habite they used in those Morrice Feasts', while another, taking their genealogy still farther back exclaims, 'The Dithyrambus was . . . a kind of extatick Morice-dance.' At the end of the eighteenth century the name still came easily to impatient lips, as when a character in a book exclaims, 'You'll be pleased to Morrice off, while you are in a whole skin!'

Up to about 1850 it was all still in full swing, altered surprisingly little in the south, for the Bampton 'side' and the Headington men who changed Cecil Sharp's life appear to-day almost precisely as their seventeenth and eighteenth predecessors appeared. In the north Midlands it developed, or perhaps retrograded, into something different, processions taking the place of normal Morris set dances, and these in full panoply and much drink accompanied the Rush Carts, while one town, Royton in Lancashire, has evolved a type of its own, unique amongst Morris dances. They, too, had left off dancing because 'nobody cared', but sprang into energetic life again directly they found interest was still taken in them. They are little, wizened cotton-spinners, well turned out in knee-breeches and black jockey caps. Their handkerchiefs are half-way to being sticks, wound round with tape into solid thongs, their Morris shoon are Lancashire clogs, and their nimble footing reminds one of Chaucer's Parish clerk, who

with his leggés casten to and fro.

They dance in an admirable pattern, two boys on the ends of the set, and their band is two accordions played in exact unison by two little old fellows, and several drums, the drummers sporting Soccer 'fan' caps. The whole company is a satisfying sight, true 'folk' and modern from heads to heels.

Besides these the amazing black-faced Bacup dancers, who still live and leap right in the heart of one of our most industrial regions, link with both the various Garland dances of Europe and *Les Cocos* of Provence. These last are supposed 'to imitate Moors', but the Bacup men repudiate the name of Morris, present themselves as 'Coco-nut dancers', and like their Provençal namesakes play upon halved coco-nuts attached to knees, elbows and breasts, as though upon castanets.

The name Morris, Morrice, or Morisco, in all of which forms and many others it appears in English literature, without any doubt whatever bears the meaning of Moorish. Our first English notice of both name and dance occurs in a will of 1458 wherein the testator mentions his 'ciphos argent sculpt cum Moreys daunce', which must have been a silver cup decorated with figures something like those in Van Mechlen's engraving (see p. 88) worked into a foliated design. Its first appearance thus coincides with the final stages of the Reconquest of Spain from the Infidel, a campaign which so stirred all Christian Europe that Moors were the great topic, and everything Moorish became the rage. This fashion for Saracens, Turks and Moors, as they were indifferently called, may be supposed to have begun in the masques and dances of Courts and noble castles, to have worked into the pageants organized by the merchant class and the town guilds, and finally to have reached the ceremonies of the country folk. German Carnival plays of the fifteenth century were called *Morriskentänze*, an Italian Masque shows Jason sowing dragons' teeth in a *Morisco*, the Rei da Mourama wormed his way into Portuguese religious processions, and the Black King of Morocco into the English Mummers' play, while right into the eighteenth century negro pages were still called blackamoors.

But these Court *Moriscos* with noblemen capering as savages were not so much a direct road to the folk Morris, as a blind alley which came to an end when the fashion had worn itself out. In that less speedy age, ignorant of air mails and wireless, lacking even roads, it may have taken a generation, say thirty years, for a song, a dress fashion, a dance or a name to percolate through to the villages. By what stages then can the name have reached country feasts before the date of the silver cup, which we remember was mentioned in 1458? The word *Morisco* supposes a Spanish origin, and it was suggested long ago that John of Gaunt's soldiers, coming home from his Spanish wars in 1387, may have been its carriers. But for ten times thirty years our armies were in Gascony, on the threshold of Spain, and English soldiers from every county went to and fro to Bayonne as now they go to and fro to Malta and Gibraltar. Throughout this long period there must have been among the people a reciprocal give and take of common things never mentioned by historians, who wrote only of wars and princely passages. It is not to be questioned that there was plenty of coming and going over the passes, and that our soldier lads must have seen *Morisca* dances with their own eyes, for they are recorded in Spain as early as the twelfth century. One notable occasion for so doing may have been the exchange of visits between Edward I and Alfonso II of Aragon, the former crossing the Somport to Jaca, the latter returning the compliment by coming to Oloron in 1288. Each King, of course, had his military retinue, and we may guess at the kind of entertainments which enlivened these meetings when we recall the fact that Aragon is still to-day a land of *Moriscas.*

But a mere name, and that a foreign one, could never have raised such multitudes of jingling companies on English soil unless there had been previously something to which it could attach itself. If we admit the probability of a Spanish origin for the name, there is no reason to extend such an origin to the dance itself, still less a Moorish one. Yet for hundreds of years the Moorish origin was not questioned, and Douce, the first scholar to concern himself with so 'low' a pastime, accepted it. The obvious difference between the English Morris and the true Moorish dances, or rather what he took the Moorish dances to be, appears to have awakened his doubts. These, however, he found easy to allay, referring to distance and the progress of such fashions through countries foreign to their nature as sufficient to explain the alterations they underwent. Even Cecil Sharp, when he published the first edition of his first *Morris Book* in 1906, did not depart from this time-honoured view, his arguments in favour of a Moorish origin being the name, the fact that the dance was found 'on both sides of the Franco-Spanish border and in a form remarkably like that with which we are familiar in England', and 'the custom observed by many Morris men of blackening their faces'.

How Sharp came to change his views six years later, and why, will be seen in the following chapter. For the moment, we admit that the customs of the Franco-Spanish border do lend considerable colour to his first view, when taken by themselves. All along the Pyrenees and on both sides of them are springtime dancers in white, decked out with bells and ribbons, flourishing sticks and handkerchiefs, not only looking like our Morris men, but doing the selfsame movements. We have seen them already, bursting out of that door in the wall.

Let us for a moment transfer ourselves to another Basque village, that of Berriz in Biscay. We are standing in the little square outside a massive Renaissance church of golden limestone. A sound of wild, shrill music on pipe and drum heralds the village dancers, all clad in white, all wearing the scarlet bérets, sash and ribbons, the leathern bell-pads of their ceremonial dress. Marching stiffly with grave, unsmiling faces, they emerge on the square preceded by their Captain carrying the green, red and white Basque standard. Drawing up in double file, they straightway execute the first figure of their dance, *Yoakundia* (the Arrival). As it finishes they suddenly crouch low on the ground, while their Captain swirls the standard round and round in great sweeping movements over their bent heads—a remarkable and impressive sight. Then follow other figures with strange-sounding names, *Zortzikoa, Ezpata Jokua, Makil Aundiak* and more, a wonderful exhibition of vigour and trained skill. The dancers clash their swords, recalling the ancient Vascones, who, according to Strabo, danced 'either together or singly, competing among themselves as to who should leap the highest'. Now they exchange their swords for clubs, or proceed to dance 'singly' in *Banakoa,* and 'together' in *Binakoa,* when they come spinning out of their ranks alone or in pairs to execute steps ornamented with amazingly high kicks, in which the body remains stiffly poised while the entire foot and ankle are seen above the level of the head. But the greatest thrill is yet to come. The village musicians strike up the final *Chonchanguillo,* on the last bars of which two dancers suddenly hoist their Captain into the air, to hold him there, horizontal and motionless above their heads, like the stiffened corpse of a sacrificial victim.

Their dance, or rather series of dances, is called *Ezpata Dantza,* the Sword dance, but it might equally well be named the Club dance, for the men use heavy sticks as much as swords, and the figures have nothing in common with the hilt-and-point Sword dance figures. Their stick and sword clashing, their meeting in the middle of the set, even minor details such as the bell-pads they wear on their calves, are more nearly allied to the Morris than to the Sword dances of England. Here then we have something which is Sword dance by name and Morris by nature. Look a little farther, and in these same Franco-Spanish border valleys we find Sword dancers using long sticks actually in hilt-and-point figures, and manufacturing the Lock from them too, and hoisting their Captain perilously upon it. We find in the very next village to one of these, a set of stick dancers doing pure Morris figures, with sticks so light and small that their title of Sword dancers appears ridiculous. Without multiplying examples which exist in scores, it seems reasonable to believe that sticks are substitutes for swords, and that therefore the distinction between Sword and Morris dances is not so hard and fast as appears.

What then of their handkerchiefs? We have seen the Royton men twist up their handkerchiefs into thongs; we know a Morris dance from Ilmington in which a *Moulinet* figure is described, using handkerchiefs almost as though they were swords held hilt and point; here in this Pyrenean land of ritual dancers is a similar *Moulinet*, and single under figures as well, passing under handkerchiefs instead of swords, and bringing the men's waist-sashes into service too, as links for the circle of dancers.

Returning home, our eyes wider open, we find that our English Sword dancers and Mummers are also Morris men, at least in name. The Revesby Mummers in 1779 were 'The Plow Boys or Morris Dancers', but their dance was a Sword dance. Earsdon, Grenoside and Winlaton Sword dancers, to choose three, call themselves Morris, and so did Perth, and so, if we may believe Sir Walter Scott, did Stirling. And all three, Sword dances, Mummers' plays and Morris, indiscriminately produce a dragon, a hobby-horse, a fool, a mysterious woman, a much-travelled doctor, a death and a resurrection. Though foremost in bearing the name, occasionally (soon after the arrival of the title) showing a Moorish personage as well, the Midland Morris now conspicuously lacks the last two essentials. A killing might be easily forgotten as sticks replaced swords, but we believe Morris men, before they were thus called, did carry swords, and certain individual Morris characters still do so. In the frontier valleys just cited we have seen them using both, and have been able to follow the transition even to handkerchiefs and sashes.

While awaiting more light on this point in our own island, the existence of some form of Sword dance may be deduced in what is now the Morris country; not the form we see to-day in the north, but with the non-dancing characters, the Fool and the Woman, and tending to drama, possibly with an animal as the central figure instead of a man. Two such rites are of so much interest and importance in Morris history that they must have a few words of description. The Kirtlington Lamb Ale continued up to 1858 and brought out a Lord and Lady, a Fool with regulation cow-tail and a bladder, a man with a live lamb on his shoulders, two people bearing 'forest feathers', which were wooden clubs entirely covered with leaves, rushes and flowers, and the six Morris dancers. The lamb was thus carried about for several days, and on the last day was killed and made into pies. The 'head pie' was greatly sought after and sold, the rest were distributed to any one lucky enough to get a piece. The Abingdon ceremony centred round an ox. Some long time ago a black ox was roasted; in 1910 and later only its horns appeared, and these were borne about on a pole. A mock Mayor, elected by the dwellers on Ox Street, was carried up and down this street on June 19th, attended by six Morris dancers and their Fool with painted face. Other indications connect the Midland Morris with animals, and one may imagine these forms of ritual decaying, frowned down as pagan, giving way under the weight of Church disapproval, and reaching vanishing point, unless fresh interest arrived from outside to renew them in different shape.

Moving gradually from the winter solstice—if they ever belonged to it—to Carnival (and Carnival which England has completely forgotten, opens with the New Year), pushed summerwards by Robin Hood and his company, these nameless dancers were finally appropriated by the great May Game. At this psychological moment they would easily accept a new name, so that when country records begin the fashionable foreign appellation is already firmly in place. Again in other lands we shall see them jingling forth all through the first half of the year, from winter to summer solstice, and, listening to the bells, to the rattle of swords, the clash of sticks, to the cries of the Fool and to the sound of a thousand dancing feet, we shall come to understand that Morris, Mummers and Sword dancers are all one great company, and that under the title of *Morisco* the three meet.

CHAPTER VI

CHRISTIANS AND MOORS

Já se renderam os Turcos,
Já se acabou toda a guerra.
(*Auto de Floripes*)
(Now the infidels have surrendered,
Now the whole war is over.)

WE were able to put forward some sort of a claim to having made the Country dance specially our own. Not so with the hilt-and-point Sword dance which appears from one end of Europe to the other, from the Middle Ages to the present day. If the Sword dance is lowly both in its supposed origin and in its present-day usage, there was a time when it went up in the world. In the Low Countries, Germany and Scandinavia, it was adopted in the fifteenth and sixteenth centuries by the Trade Guilds, especially those of the Shoemakers and Metalworkers, and done by them with great skill and solemnity, usually at Carnival time.

It is of these urban, middle-class Sword dances rather than of those done by peasants that, not unnaturally, we find the earliest mention. The first authenticated reference to such a dance concerns one done at Bruges at Carnival time in 1389. With the turn of the century they follow thick and fast, until the gradual decay of the Guilds resulted in the virtual extinction of the Sword dance in the towns. But the villages took back, perhaps in a slightly more elaborate form, what they had originally given to the cities, and the Sword dance lived on in the country, as numerous references testify, through the eighteenth and nineteenth centuries. It is still seen to-day in south Germany and Austria and among the scattered communities of German settlers as far east as Siebenbürgen in Roumania. In Austria alone Dr. Richard Wolfram has found a wide variety of different Sword dances, from Hallein near Salzburg (where the dance is the particular property of the workers in the salt mine), as far as the borders of Yugoslavia and Hungary.

These Sword dances of northern and central Europe closely resemble the English ones. Like ours they have the circle, the clash, the single-over and single-under, and, most important of all, the Lock which, as in parts of England, is called the Rose. Some, indeed, are considerably more elaborate, and include a ' bridge ' figure as in *Oranges and*

Lemons, and a maze figure in which the dancers wind into a tight spiral and then unwind again. Almost invariably the climax of the dance is reached when the Captain (who does not dance but acts as a Presenter) or the Leader is hoisted into the air on the Rose of interlocked swords, and salutes the assembled company. It is difficult to interpret this hoisting with any certainty, but it may perhaps be regarded as a resurrection, for the Rose is generally supported by the Fool, or, as in our dances, is actually plaited round his neck. So the Fool 'dies' and the Captain or Leader is raised up, just as in the play (which in Germany and Austria as in England often accompanies the dance) some one is invariably killed and brought to life by the Doctor.

An old drawing of the Sword dance at Nuremberg, of which some of the earliest descriptions are by Hans Sachs, shows two Leaders, each hoisted on a separate Rose, fighting with broadswords, a suggestion of a combat which it will be convenient to bear in mind.

Generally, however, these hilt-and-point Sword dances contain nothing to suggest a combat. Obviously, swords were not primarily designed to serve as links in an unbroken chain of dancers, and the hilt-and-point figure is neither a normal nor even a convenient use to which to put them. If it were not for the obvious indications of a ceremonial killing, we might be tempted to wonder whether the swords were not later substitutes for the leather thongs, sticks or hoop-shaped garlands with which exactly similar dances were, and still are, danced in the same regions. Thus at Ulm in the year 1551 boys danced the Sword dance in the daytime and the Garland dance at night. In the latter 'each one had half a green hoop in his hand. And the figures were the same as the Sword dance.'

With just such hoops I saw men and (exceptionally) women from Aussee in the Salzkammergut do precisely similar figures culminating in the *Häusl*, a bower formed of interlaced garlands as the Rose is formed of interlaced swords.

The most famous of these Garland dances is the *Schäfflertanz* of Munich, done every seven years by the Coopers' Guild, and performed in January 1935 before the Duke and Duchess of Kent. There are seven figures in all. In the first, called the *Schlange*, the twenty-five dancers wind in and out until the box-covered half-hoops which they carry form a snake, after which they perform the *Laube* (or Arcade), the *Kreuz* (Cross) and the *Krone*, one of the prettiest and most complicated of the figures, in which the half-hoops form a crown. Next come the *Kleiner Kreis* and *Chassieren* in which the dancers respectively break into four separate smaller circles, and advance and retire in lines. The seventh and last figure is the *Reifenschwung*, a grand finale in which a large circle is formed round two dancers, who swing in their fingers a small hoop bearing a tumbler of wine. The whole dance lasts about twenty minutes and is executed with a polka step the whole way through.

This is the last survivor of a large number of similar dances performed by the Guilds at longish intervals. Thus at Frankfort the coopers used to dance on the frozen River Main, and from Braunau the cutlers and armourers came to Munich every eight years and performed a Sword dance by imperial charter before the houses of the city notables. The origins of the *Schäfflertanz* are lost in obscurity, but it seems to have started in the year of some great plague such as 1350, 1462, 1517 or 1634, and in spite of a legend that it was invented to cheer the people up, its intention was more probably propitiatory. The first year in which it is recorded with any certainty is 1669. In 1683, two seven-year cycles later, the accounts of Kurfurst Max Emanuel show a payment of three guilders to the *Schäffler* for their dance. In the same year the account-books of his uncle, Duke Max Philip, contain an entry relating to the '*Schäffler* who *fenced* at this Palace on Shrove Tuesday', which suggests that the dance was then a Sword dance. The music is not very ancient, nor are the present costumes, which are said to have been designed by King Ludwig II of Bavaria. These consist of red jackets, black satin knee-breeches, white stockings, white aprons folded half-way back over the right leg, and black caps with blue and white plumes. The dancers are accompanied by two Fools, and carry a small barrel and a flag with a device in the Munich city colours.

We may probably take it for granted that the Garland dance was a development of the Sword dance rather than vice versa, and that the intermediate stage was that in which swords were replaced by sticks. At Zeche in the Slovakian Carpathians, where swords are replaced by thin hazel-rods, Dr. Wolfram noted that these were used straight at first, but bent to typical half-hoops in the middle of the dance. In the Catalan *Cercollets* the Captain is actually hoisted on the intertwined garlands of his dancers as elsewhere he is on their Lock of swords.

Dr. Wolfram's theories on the origins of the Sword dance appear at first sight to conflict with those generally held, for he derives it, not from agricultural fertility rites, but from initiation ceremonies handed down by secret societies of men. To these he ascribes not only the dance itself but its by-play. 'In most of our Sword and Garland dances', he writes, 'the Fool is first of all shaved in a comic way. Then follows another procedure, the extraction of a tooth. . . . Then he drops down dead and is revived again by all sorts of ridiculous means. Again in other Sword dances the Fool is killed in the dance either by fencing or by the "lock" . . . . If we examine the rites of admittance (i.e. to men's societies) we find shaving and tooth-extraction. . . .' It is true that death and resurrection play an important part in such initiation rites, the child being imagined as dying and the youth rising again as a new man; and that such secret societies are not yet extinct in the Austrian Alps where one of them is still responsible for the *Schemenlaufen* of Imst, of which we shall hear more. But Sword dances are inextricably bound up with the calendar, whereas, if one may judge from the analogy of modern rites of initiation in savage countries, this ceremony is rarely if ever governed by seasons. Moreover, need such societies have been the actual inventors of their initiation rites? May they not more probably have adapted to this end ancient ceremonies of more general character, of which the men, and especially the young unmarried ones, are invariably the traditional hierophants?

The principal authority on these dances is the German, Karl Meschke, whose theories, however, are as ill-considered as his accumulation of material is valuable. By dint of leaving out of consideration almost all the non-German Sword dances and concentrating on the dance at the expense of its attendant mumming fragments, he contrives to invest it with an exclusively German character and to trace it back through Tacitus, who described a Sword dance of the German tribes performed in the first century A.D. by naked young men, to prehistoric cave-drawings.

Yet in their own Germanic world Meschke and Wolfram had before them the evidences which link the Sword dance directly with agricultural fertility rites. At Hochweis in the Carpathians, the Fool of the Sword dances is completely covered in straw like our own Jack-in-the-Green. On Shrove Tuesday he must dance with his hostess so that the year may be fertile, and then he jumps over the swords. As high as he jumps so high will the corn grow. In the Boehmerwald two Fools accompany the dancers. Their clothes are covered by innumerable little patches which the peasant women tear off their backs in the belief that if they put them under the hens the latter will lay better.

With the exception of those once existing in Holland, it cannot even be claimed that many Sword dances are to be found on the fringes of the German-speaking world. How can German theories account for the famous *Bacubert* in the Dauphiné, France, and for its appearance with a Sword dance play at Fenestrelle, Piedmont, and in countries so far away as Poland, Czechoslovakia, Bulgaria, Yugoslavia, Spain and Portugal? Yet in all of these, hilt-and-point Sword dances are found in close association with those rites which folklorists tell us spring from the oldest and most urgent needs of humanity.

On the tiny island of Lagosta (Lastovo) in the Adriatic, to which German influence can scarcely have penetrated, a Sword dance is associated with very curious Carnival celebrations. The dancers are dressed in dark clothes and hats adorned with flowers and ribbons. They take round a straw 'guy' called *Poklad* (Carnival) on a gaily caparisoned donkey to the houses of the village notables. Then, to the accompaniment of cheers, they throw him over a precipice. In the evening after the hilt-and-point figures of their dance, they pull their puppet to pieces and burn him, so that the spirit of Carnival, a sacrificial victim here as everywhere else, is killed not once but twice.

In the last chapter we saw that by the time we reach the Pyrenees, Sword dance and Morris can scarcely be distinguished. Throughout southern Europe, hilt-and-point figures, if present at all, are less the central feature of the dance than in Germany, less its end-all-and-be-all. Not that there is any lack of them. A Sword dance near Toledo used to conclude (and still may do) with a lock formed round the throat of one of the dancers who then escapes. That the meaning of the figure may not be for one moment in doubt it is called *La Degollada* (The

Beheading). The Captain of the Biscayan Sword dancers used to be hoisted on a lock at Marquina, as his opposite number at Fenestrelle or Ibio is to-day. But in these northern Spanish dances hilt-and-point figures are often quite subsidiary to the tapping or clashing figures which we may call Pyrrhic. In the Basque province of Guipúzkoa the dancers tap with decorated half-hoops, which must originally have been intended to serve as links, as in the German Garland dances.

When we were speculating on the origins of the Morris dance in the last chapter we saw that Cecil Sharp, having accepted the theory of a Moorish origin, came later to reject it. His principal reason for doing so was that by 1912 he had come to realize that all over Europe the dance does not stand by itself, but is associated with 'certain strange customs which are apparently quite independent of the dance itself'. From this he concluded that 'the Morris dance is a development of a pan-European or even more widely extended custom', and that 'the faces were not blackened because the dancers represented Moors, but rather the dancers were thought to represent Moors because their faces were blackened'.

It never occurred to Sharp to connect the Morris dance with the numerous ceremonial combats between 'Christians' and 'Moors', all more or less choreographic in form, which are found throughout southern Europe, from Dalmatia in the east to Portugal in the west. Perhaps he had no opportunity of hearing of them, but a connection with the Morris is evident from their appellation of *Morisca, Morisma, Moreška, Mouriscada* or some similar name.

The *Moreška*, performed every year in September in the Dalmatian island of Korčula (Curzola), consists of a play and Sword dance representing a combat between two groups of dancers, a White King (Christian) contending with a Black King (Moorish) for the hand of a beautiful slave called Bula. Needless to say, as in all such mock-battles, the Christians emerge victorious.

In Spain, the battle of Moors and Christians goes back at least to the twelfth century, one such having been performed in 1137 at the betrothal of Count Ramon Berenguer of Barcelona and Queen Petronila of Aragon. Aragon, as has already been stated, is still to-day a land of *Morisca* dances, and few more striking performances could be found than the *Morisma* of Ainsa. This takes place in the middle of September every year and has a dramatis personae comprising over twenty characters, including Christian and Moorish Kings, Queens and Ambassadors. On the morning of September 14th the two armies, Christian and Moorish, march out of the village by separate roads. Mass is celebrated outside the village at the

Cross of Sobrarbe, and is watched from a distance by the jeering 'Moors'. After the recital of the Prologue the Kings address imperious challenges to one another, and there follow two battles, the first at Sobrarbe and the other in the main square of Ainsa. I am told that these battles take the form of stick dances, though I have not actually seen them. After an interval for the midday meal there are *pourparlers* between the Ambassadors, after which battle is joined for the third time, the Cross is made to appear miraculously in the middle of the *Plaza Mayor,* and the Moorish King is taken prisoner and executed. The Christians fall to their knees with a hymn of thanksgiving, and Moorish soldiers fall dead around them. The remainder accept baptism, and the festival concludes on the following day with a prostration before the Cross of Sobrarbe and the recital of an Epilogue.

The stage of the *Morisma* is the whole village of Ainsa, but other *Moriscas* have been dramatically stylized in the form of a play such as the *Auto de Floripes,* which is performed once a year on the occasion of a pilgrimage to the shrine of Our Lady of the Snows, at Souto das Neves near Barcelos in northern Portugal. The subject is the warfare between Charlemagne with his Twelve Peers, and the Moors under Admiral Balão, with the rivalry of Oliver and Fierabras for the hand of the Moorish

Princess Floripes as a subsidiary theme. King Ismar, the latter's father, carries a jester's bauble, and this, combined with his comic rôle, suggests that he derives from an earlier Fool like the one who accompanies so many Morris and Sword dance teams.

In 1932, when I saw the play, the stage was of boards laid across barrels, the only backcloth being the green hills beside the River Lima. At each end was a sort of draped sentry-box crowned, the one with a Christian and the other with an Ottoman standard. In the centre, on the frontier as it were, stood a drummer who marked with a drum-beat or prolonged roll the most important events of the play. The Christians wore blue coats, white trousers and yachting-caps, and carried muskets. The Moors, armed with swords, wore rich crimson robes, and tall, cylindrical hats. The frequent battles with which the play was interspersed were more like dances than a realistic representation of fighting, and at the end, when Oliver had gone off with his masculine Floripes, the principal characters danced a sort of 'Three Meet' Country dance figure which concluded the proceedings.

In the Basque *Pastorales* the stylization of the battle of Moors and Christians is carried one stage farther. These are outdoor plays, purely medieval in technique, in which, whatever the subject, whether biblical, historical or legendary, the characters are divided into two camps who are called Christians and Turks, although in point of fact they may be Israelites and Canaanites, Medes and Persians or, in a recent example dealing with the Great War, French and Germans. In the *Pastorale* of Joan of Arc the English are the Turks, who are invariably shown by their costume to be pure Morris dancers with little switches and tall head-dresses decked with flowers and mirrors. Once again the numerous battles are no combats but rudimentary Sword dances to the accompaniment of music.

Such battles are not always between Christians and Moors or Turks. One which we shall shortly see is between Moors and 'Buffoons', and another between Portuguese and Spaniards. Can it be that the secular warfare between Christian and Infidel is not really essential to the ceremonial battle, and that it has been grafted on to a combat still more ancient? Our own Isle of Man supplies what may prove to be an answer to this question. Till about a hundred years ago on May Day the Manx people used to elect not only the usual Queen of the May or of Summer, but a Queen of Winter as well. Each was attended by maidens, and by a dozen stalwart male retainers. Those of the Queen of Summer wore red cockades, whence the song *Tappaghyn Jiargey* or *Red Top-knots*. The Queen of Winter and her court wore heavy winter clothing and sprigs of evergreen. The two armies fought a mock battle in which, after many vicissitudes, such as the capture and ransom of the Queen of Summer, the forces of Winter were put to flight just as, in more southern lands, are the hordes of the Infidel. Such battles between Summer and Winter used also to be known in Austria.

From this it might appear that the afterthought (under the influence of history) of converting one of the opposing armies into Moors, in a battle which was originally between Summer and Winter, would alone account for the name of *Morisca* or Moorish being applied to a dance which, as Sharp came to recognize, never had anything to do with the Moors. But this would leave out of account the fact that many, indeed most, Morris dances consist not of two but only of one group of dancers, and that the killing in both *Moriscas* and Sword dances is not the indiscriminate slaughter of battle but the solemn slaying of an annual sacrificial victim. We have mentioned that Sharp came round to the view that the faces of the dances were not blackened because they were thought to represent Moors, but that they were thought to represent Moors because their faces were blackened. Why, then, were their faces blackened?

The answer is not far to seek. All over Europe, wherever the diversions of the folk go back to seasonal ceremonies once performed in desperate earnest, we find that the celebrants of the rites must be disguised or masked in order that they may not be recognizable as familiar members of the community. For this reason Cornish 'guisers', Austrian Carnival runners, Bacup Coco-nut dancers, and all their kin either wear masks, or disguise their honest country faces with lamp-black, and are thereby transformed into blackamoors.

It has recently been shown,[1] moreover, that in various parts of the Iberian Peninsula, the term Moorish has come to be used almost as a synonym of 'pagan', being applied in Portugal both to pre-Christian archaeological remains and to babies who die unbaptized. There are, therefore, not one but several reasons to account for the name of Moorish having come to be applied quite wrongly and misleadingly to something which existed long before the Moslem hordes overran Europe.

Before we close this chapter, let us see what is perhaps the strangest of all these continental 'Mauresque' performances, the *Mouriscada* performed annually at Sobrado near Valongo (Portugal) which the authors of this book saw together in 1932, and the existence of which had till then been unknown even to Portuguese folklorists.

[1] *The Origins of the Morris Dance,* by Rodney Gallop, in *The Journal of the English Folk Dance and Song Society,* Vol. I, No. 3.

We reached the little village among the pines and vineyards near the Douro at about six o'clock in the evening of Midsummer Day. A village green sloped down from the high road to a white church backed by a wooded hill-side, vivid in the slanting rays of the sun. We had missed the earlier part of the performance which begins at midday when the *Mouriscos* (Moors) and the *Bugios* (Buffoons) effect their ceremonial entry into the village. At the churchyard gate they are met by the Sacristan holding a vessel of holy water which he offers to the two 'Kings', together with a branch of olive with which each of these asperges his kneeling men. Then follows a curious pantomime, which smells strongly of midsummer magic. One of the *Bugios* rides into the village, seated back to front on a pony and sowing flax. The ground where he passes is next harrowed and lastly ploughed with two donkeys whose yoke is put on upside down so that it hangs beneath their chins. Before they reach the village green the plough must fall to pieces, so that everything is thus done in inverse order.

We had not timed our arrival too badly, however, for the dances which are the prelude to the performance proper had just begun. With drawn swords, to the hilts of which were knotted clean white handkerchiefs, the *Mouriscos* were dancing in the trellised courtyard of the priest's house. They wore light-coloured cotton suits, with golden buttons and belts and sashes. On their heads were cardboard shakos a foot high, hung with little mirrors and gold braid, and surmounted with red plumes. They faced each other in two long files as in a Longways Country dance. The King, distinguished by gold chains and epaulettes, danced down the middle, and then the top couple 'cast off' outwards, followed by all the rest, met at the bottom and came up the middle in pairs. Now and again the King led them into a 'snail' for which they formed single file, and then unravelling themselves, separated into two files, one led by the King, one by the vice-King, before returning to meet face to face. The only music was the monotonous beating of a drum, which combined with the silence and purposeful air of the dancers to lend their performance an uncommunicably ominous quality, such as might presage some outburst of savage warfare.

Finally the *Mouriscos* danced out of the yard and the *Bugios* danced in. As they came down the fair-ground led by their King, they leapt, howled and threw their arms about. They were incongruously dressed in faded velvet cloaks with tinsel trimmings, knee-breeches with frills at the knee, and huge hats with paper fringes at the brim and showers of streamers hanging from the crown, like those of the Overton Mummers. They were hung with small

PORTUGUESE MOURISCOS AT SOBRADO

EL DANCE AT SENA, ARAGON

bells and had castanets in their pockets, and household or agricultural implements in their hands. All except the King were masked, some in ordinary Carnival faces, others as animals, and one at least in a primitive and horrible mask, home-made out of cork-bark. Their King had exercised his traditional privilege of choosing his costume from among the Church vestments. He wore a crimson damask cope arranged like a mantle, and had added a lace frill round his shoulders.

The dance which now began was even more extraordinary than that which had preceded it. The top couple, paper plumes waving, arms going like windmills, rushed at their King, sometimes bent at the waist with hands on their knees, sometimes almost crouching. With the sinister swaying gestures of a necromancer their Lord appeared to be giving them secret and nefarious orders. Then with an upward sweep of the arms he dismissed the cowering figures, and a turn and a flying leap carried them to the end of the line. All this was done to a little scrap of melody for two fiddles and a guitar, repeated again and again with almost hynotic monotony.

Then the second part of the *Mouriscada* began. Two small wooden platforms had been erected on the village green about eighty yards apart. In these 'castles' the two Kings took their stand, each accompanied by a few chosen retainers, and began to send mounted Ambassadors to one another with defiant messages. As each 'Ambassador' started on his errand the warriors fired a salvo with muzzle-loading muskets and leapt high into the air.

This went on till it was eight o'clock and the sun was low on the horizon. Then came a moment when the *Bugios* had exhausted their powder and could defend themselves no longer. The *Mouriscos* formed up and marched to the attack of the 'castle'. Twice they assaulted it and twice they were beaten back. The third time, led by their King, they swarmed successfully up the ladder. There was a brief mêlée on the small platform, and the *Rei Bugio*, masked now, was seen sheltering beside his men. A moment later the Moorish King found him and smote him to the ground. A sudden hush fell. The fallen monarch sat up, and his followers came in turn to bid him a tearful farewell with tender embraces. Then, with an imperious gesture, his captor bade him descend the steps, the *Mouriscos* formed a close phalanx, and to the strains of a funeral march he was led away. The vanquished company hovered on the outskirts moaning and lamenting.

For a moment we were carried far away in space and time. Were we not beholding with our own eyes the age-old procession of the dead Osiris? And if this was so, should we not also witness his liberation from the bonds of death? The answer was not long in coming. There was a sudden diversion in a far corner of the green. From beneath their 'castle' a party of *Bugios* had dragged out a monstrous *Bicha* (serpent or dragon) about eight feet long, made of sacking over a light wooden frame and painted with large spots. His tail was a fir branch, his tongue of red cotton. With hair-raising cries the *Bugios* ran with him into the crowd, making him rear and dart, till they reached the approaching and still lamenting procession. Then they loosed him. With well-simulated terror the *Mouriscos* fled, leaving their prisoner to be rescued by his men and led away in triumph.

The dead Osiris had risen again, and now, the mumming over, there remained only the *dança do santo* to give a Christian finish to the ceremony. Once again the two teams went through their weird dances, this time in front of the church and in honour of St. John, thus bringing to a close one of the strangest survivals in the whole of Europe.

CHAPTER VII

'LONG WOODEN IDOLS'

'I have a mighty retinue,
The scum of all the rascal crew;
My summons fetcheth far and near
All that can swagger, roar and swear,
All that can dance, and drab and drink,
They run to me as to a sink.'

(*Puritan pamphlet*)

THUS spoke the Maypole. Where, then, are the lads who, so dutifully taking leave of their Dads, away to the Maypole hied? Where are the apple-cheeked lassies, who not too inelegantly did

trip it, trip it,
trip it to the men,

and the meek old fiddler, and the innocuous cakes in the bower? This is a different picture indeed from the one we have accustomed ourselves to visualize, but probably nearer the truth. It was sketched by a Puritan hand, of course, that of a

Roundhead pastor, who took the place of the legal Anglican Rector in those uncomfortable Commonwealth days, but who, when this diatribe was published, must have been near the end of his usurpation, for it was the Maypole re-erected in Cheapside after the King had come to his own again that inspired his hymn of hate. Let us see if the virulent cleric finds corroboration.

The earliest Maypoles known with certainty are both in the north, in John's reign at Lostock near Bolton, 'where the cross was formerly', and in 1373 at Pendleton, that village afterwards so famous for witches. Both may be looked upon as fairly modern examples, the longest part of their genealogy already behind them. In 1244 or thereabouts, Grosseteste, Bishop of Lincoln, felt it his duty to do something about Maypoles, and issued a decree forbidding the May Game, but it could not have had much effect, for those lines quoted about 'Caroles, somour games and many shames' belong to the year 1303, and the writer of them believed, like the Bishop, that he was 'handling sin'. Then, unable to suppress the Maypole, the Church in some degree adopted it, swept it into her own jurisdiction, as she did so many questionable old things, paid out money for it, and even accepted money from it. Church accounts all through the sixteenth and seventeenth centuries show such entries as the bell-ringer cleansing the church at the ‘ dance of poles ’, another man getting fourpence for ‘ XXIIII grete nails ’ for the ‘ dance of poles ’, and a carpenter spending two days making a ladder of the Maypole—an old one presumably. The actual ‘ felling and bringing home the bough ’ was paid for, and when the Church approved, the King approved too, for we see Henry VII giving as much as ten shillings to Lambeth girls ‘ for a May ’, and contributing to the May Game in Greenwich Park. Henry VIII was an adept at maying, and it was in his reign that the great Maypole was erected on Cornhill, so high that it out-topped the steeple of the church nearby, and gave it the name of St. Andrew Undershaft. There were lesser poles all over London, and Morris dances, and May Games, and bonfires in the streets, all organized by ‘ the governors and masters of the city ’, and therefore respectable enough—at least while the City Fathers looked on.

Now records multiply, yet the Maypole itself is taken for granted, and all the information is about the Morris and Robin Hood. The original bearer of this name—if there ever were one in reality, for he grows more and more mythical—was supposed to have lived his outlawed life in the reign of Henry II. His village representative began to appear in verse and the Games at the very opening of the fourteenth century, and in the next hundred years became so firmly fixed that we cannot be rid of him. Sir John Paston's groom acted in a Robin Hood play in 1473, while down in the most rural part of Somerset they 'presented in the spoil of Roburt Hode and his Company' for many years, the church funds profiting, but some of the money being spent on furbishing up the actors. At Kingston-on-Thames, for instance, two shillings had to be spared out of the spoil for sponging and brushing Robin Hood's coat. This character, founded on a legendary figure, had an exceedingly curious rise to fame. He worked his way into the affections of the people, annexed the midland and southern ritual dancers, and finally crowned himself King of the May.

Yet he could not have been essential to the May Game, for we frequently find him 'gathering' for himself, and when his play and the May Game were held together at Kingston, it is specially remarked that one 'gathering' was made for both. They both enjoyed a long period, perhaps two hundred years, of unmolested popularity, until new Puritanical ideas pounced upon them right in the middle of what we now call Merry England days. Scottish divines, too, threw themselves into the fray, sourly writing of the 'rascal multitude stirred up to make a Robin Hude', and even arraigning people for 'fetching home a Maypole and dancing about the same'.

Stubbs, whose vivid picture of the Morris we saw in a previous chapter, flew at the Maypole in a fury, agreeing with the writer whose epithet heads this chapter, and the 'long wooden idols', the 'stinking idols', the 'heathenish vanities', were all hacked down when the Roundheads worked their will on old England. Apart from these extravagant pens, a grave Lancashire magistrate calls the May Games 'lewd sports', and it is well known there was ground for apprehension, not so much in the dancing and games which were held in public under the eyes of the whole village, as in the preparations for the great day. These necessitated going out into the woods and fields to find greenery and flowers, and it is an established fact that the Mayers made a night of it, girls and men together, taking all the licence traditionally allowed at the great pre-Christian feast of the Renewal of Nature. A private, human touch, very different from the stream of vehemence, adds to the evidence. 'Papists' were suspected of providing Maypoles and upholding the Games; here, a Roman Catholic writing of the Maypole in his diary, adds in the margin, 'Ne reminiscaris Domine delicta juventutis mea.'

So, making allowance for Puritan hatred, it does seem as though the drabbing, swaggering and swearing picture were the right one. We made the other picture for ourselves, out of ballads composed by townspeople who admired Phillis and Corydon from a distance, but the folk themselves, in their own May Carol, give the truth simply and without comment.

> Oh, we've been rambling all this night
> And some time of this day,
> And now we're coming home again
> To bring you in the May.

Like the Mummers they *have to.*

In spite of support from the Stuart Kings and the setting up of the poles again at the Restoration, the May Games dwindled away, and only a few old poles managed to stand upright through the nineteenth century. At Downham in Lancashire, the Game with the King and Queen, dancing, and the 'Queen's Posset' as the feast was called, went on long after surrounding villages had learnt to despise their own festivities, and in the rural parts of Cotswold several remained to figure in Morris ceremonies. The Ducklington Morris performed *Green Garters,* that charming processional still to be seen at Bampton, round their pole previous to a day's dancing, and once forgetting to do so were called back by an infuriated old man who, considering the pole insulted, threatened to cut it down. Men only, but half of them dressed as women, formed the ring round the Syresham pole, and Offenham's pole was decorated annually up to 1912.[1] Now, the last stage of decrepitude, miniature poles are carried about by children, and the old song, also in decrepitude, is sung as an excuse for a 'gathering'.

> All around the Maypole, trit, trit, trot,
> What a funny Maypole we have got.

Funny, indeed, and a sad come down from thirty feet of strong birch stem to a stick picked up in the lane, with a dirty ribbon round it.

On Cooper's Hill behind Gloucester stands a tall, slim pole, to which comes a crowd of eager people every Whit Monday. The 'Master', in full Morris dress, white shirt, ribbons and bells, tall white hat and authority, sets off a cheese—an imitation Double Gloucester—on a headlong career down the steep pitch into the valley. Everybody rushes after it; the winner gets a real cheese and one or two losers a broken leg, a band plays, and modern dancing goes on into the evening. They could not dance round the Maypole if they wanted to, for it is set too near the edge of the green precipice. Regular Cheese Bowlers who have raced ever since they could run, scorn 'them up-country people' whose cars block the woodland tracks, and laugh at the recent broadcast.

It will now be seen that although a good deal is

[1] From Cecil Sharp's unpublished notes.

known about Maypoles, hardly anything is known about Maypole dances. It cannot even be said whether the plaiting of the pole be 'traditional' like a folk song, or 'composed' like a popular one. It is certain that up to now no reliable mention of plaiting has been found, nor does any picture show it except purely fancy ones, or in some arranged Masque. At Slingsby, Yorkshire, the children plait an ancient Maypole on Old May Day, but this is the direct handiwork of the schoolmistress. It is because we connect plaiting with school children that we look at it askance, yet it cannot be asserted that it is entirely fanciful, for we shall presently see grown men plaiting a pole at full speed. Meanwhile, we will glance at the 'Maypoles all the way down Sheep Street, and people dancing round them wearing oak leaves', as recounted by an old Herefordshire woman, and at the 'Men and girls dancing the Maypole dance hand in hand in a ring' in Lancashire. This clearly takes us back to the *Carole,* that early form of ring dance from which sprang the round Country dance. Of these Rounds we possess plenty which might have been Maypole dances, but again we know only one that was certainly thus used. This is *Sellenger's Round* or *The Beginning of the World,* a favourite which swings grandly round the circular floor of the Albert Hall every winter, when English dances have a night of their own at the English Folk Dance

Festival. Three hundred or more white-clad men and brightly frocked girls form great concentric circles round a Jack-in-the-Green, who makes a living Maypole in the middle. A heartening sight it is, and a heartening sound too is the rhythmic, heavy old tune, accompanying the eight slips sun-wise and the eight slips back, and the breaking off to step up into the middle between each arming, siding and setting to partners. Here at last is something we are certain of, for this was 'danced in moonshine nights about Maypoles', as long ago as Elizabeth's dancing days and before them. It appears again in a 'Garland' of tunes, with a woodcut of men and women in a hands-all ring round a Maypole, and to make assurance doubly sure is marked 'Hey for Sellenger's Round'. The tune was harmonized by Byrd for the so-called *Queen Elizabeth's Virginal Book,* so it must have been popular in Court and village alike. *Gathering Peascods,* with its swinging rings and its running into the middle as though to touch something invisible there, is surely an early Maypole dance—I do not speak of the tune—but it is internal evidence only that tells us so. The lassies who began this chapter did

> jet it, jet it,
> jet it in and out,

which sounds as though they heyed (the grand

chain) past the men, the expression, incidentally, being perhaps a corruption of the ballet term *jeté*; and this, with constant references to somewhat violent gambols, to leaping and springing, is all the technical information we possess about Maypole dances in the British Isles.

So we cross the water in search of more, and will choose the North Sea first, hoping for smooth blue stretches on a midsummer day, for Maypoles have moved on a month in these latitudes. Swedish Midsummer poles are famous, and an amusing sight it is to watch people flocking out of the towns towards evening on the day which has no night. Nowadays large numbers of women and girls wear the crude reds and blues and yellows of regional dresses, each demurely carrying a wrap over her arm, for although as light as day midnight will be chilly. Care must be taken to avoid known gatherings such as those of Dalecarlia, which are flooded out with native and foreign tourists, where the costumes are worn by 'Youth' societies, and the dances performed by folk dance associations. But there is real stuff still to be seen, a *Gōd Midsomer* still to be enjoyed.

Finnish Maypoles are gorgeous, reaching up into the sky, shining with tinsel, and encircled on midsummer night by rings of dancers. But again there is not much to be said of the dance itself, for nothing can be simpler nor require less description than a hand-in-hand ring. We might wander all over Europe looking at May and Midsummer, Easter and Whitsuntide poles, picking out such interesting examples as the Czech tree dressed in white, and carried triumphantly about by girls, while at the same time a disreputable guy is carried by the boys. After all the bad treatment they can devise, this personage is thrown violently into water. I saw him go into a duck pond, and a glorious splash went up, the ducks flapped and squawked, the drops hung about afterwards like diamonds in the clear mid-European sunlight, and the little girls scuttled away from the scene of execution like a flock of white ducks themselves, carrying with them their own unsullied, dressed-up birch sapling—only the one I saw was a doll. A more delightful sight can hardly be imagined on an early spring morning, nor a more ancient one, for what they sing is their farewell to 'Death' or Winter, their welcome to Summer and its warmth and pleasures.

Not far off, in the province of Moravia, a great Maypole goes up in October, moved away from its proper date by political reasons of long ago. Under it men gather in their gay embroidered dress, and at the command of their Master of the Ceremonies step out one by one to dance a *pas seul* beneath the pole. Here we see something different from the usual ring, and the motif of the dance is as old as the throwing of Winter into the pond—they jump as high as possible to make the crops grow tall.

Coming westwards again through the Alps, it will be worth while going up the valley to Champéry beneath the towering points of the Dent du Midi, to have a look at the Maypole, erected there in high summer, when the snow has withdrawn up the slopes and the pastures are as green as fresh lettuces. They come out in their valley costume, these Swiss Mayers, men in knee-breeches and cutaway coats, white stockings and tall hats, women in full skirts and fuller aprons, on their heads queer, hard, high hats with pleats of ribbon round them, more ribbons falling down their backs. This costume is of the Tyrolese, that is the central Alpine, type, and not so ancient as is generally supposed, for the Swiss regional dresses appeared only in the seventeenth and eighteenth centuries, strange as it seems to preconceived notions of their antiquity. Country dances, two and two, up a double and back a double, set to partners and turn, hands on hips—the old figures, very likely journeyed here from England—that is what goes on beneath this Valaisian pole, so we leave them to their curtsy and bow finale and cross the frontier to France.

La Douce France, never more lovely than on a May morning and in the soft south-west. For it is the old province of Gascony which to-day rears up her Maypoles as thick as forest trees. Towards Auch and that ancient town, Lectoure, you come upon them in every village; round Dax, amongst the sombre fir forests, you need but walk out of the town to find them. They are fir poles here of course, twenty or thirty feet high, bearing a bush of lighter green at the top, flags, and often a number of bottles swinging round on strings, catching the sun and acting as Aeolian harps in the fresh wind blowing in from the Atlantic. These poles were never hacked down nor persecuted by reformers, unless indeed local Huguenots tried their hands on them. If so they did not succeed, for May Queens have only just gone out of fashion, and dancing goes on gaily, modern dancing needless to say, yet often beginning or ending with a good old Gascon Round. These are the *Rondes Fermées,* and are generally sung by women unless the village is lucky enough to own an old *vielle,* a hurdy-gurdy played with a handle. One good Ronde puts a man in the middle beneath the pole. At a certain bar in the tune he dances in front of the lady of his choice, kisses her and stands in the ring beside her. Out she then goes and does the same to any man she fancies. *La Chouade,* the Oats, is charming, everybody copying the actions of sowing, cutting, tying in sheaves, finally resting—a first cousin to our *Oats and Beans and Barley Grow,* which now, in a more sophisticated land, has come down to the children.

All this time the sun is westering, lighting up more and more brilliantly the far-off Pyrenean peaks. On the other side of the snows old ways live on still more hardily than on the French slopes, and a very short journey takes us to the Basque provinces and the plaited Maypole already mentioned. This pole is one of the reasons against putting aside plaiting as something invented for children. It appears as the last figure in one of the famous Basque Sword dances, that of the province of Guipúzkoa, and the men who plait it are strong, agile fellows, racing round at full tilt, narrowly avoiding collisions which would be terrific indeed, scowling at each other if they touch, and altogether putting such a different complexion on the figure that *Cinta Dantza*, the *Ribbon Dance*, assumes another meaning. Their drums beat a furious encouragement, their three-holed pipes shrill out a gay 6/8 air, and the man in the middle holding the pole, has a strenuous time, bracing himself for the onslaught, feet well apart. Some little way farther down the Cantabrian coast a Maypole is raised in August, to suit the fair of San Lorenzo. It seems to be a very sacred pole, is put up at the hour of high mass, and remains all through the fair. When night falls people flock to it, but do nothing so frivolous as dance round it. Instead they uncover their heads while a special song is sung, bow to their pole and throw it down. In Portugal they follow northern ideas and raise their poles at midsummer, for St. John the Baptist is their particular saint and the poles are said to be St. John's poles. I came upon a beauty one hot midsummer day, reared by the roadside, entirely covered with flowers, nailed (one supposed) in stripes winding up the pole; a pink stripe of carnations, a yellow stripe of great marquerite heads, a white one of moon daisies, while over all swayed a little 'St. John', a puppet tied to the top.

Right across Spain on the Mediterranean coast, another pole is plaited, which again underlines the fact that this is something other than fancy drill for the infants' school. The mountains of Catalonia are sprinkled fairly thickly with Maypoles, but the plaited one is ambulatory like that of the Basque Sword dancers, and like theirs belongs to a company of dancers. A strong fellow in the Catalan scarlet *barretina*—a Phrygian cap of liberty—bears it about, the posse of 'Gipsies', as they call themselves, space themselves out very beautifully about him as escort, some holding the ends of the ribbons, others taking their places singly in the pattern. When the *Cobla* band strikes up, strident and inflammatory (these bands contain special regional instruments and give forth a special sound never heard elsewhere), the pole is brought to earth, and the plaiting begins, men and girls placed alternately, the single dancers still alone, performing *pas seuls* outside the circling group. Then all is undone, after which the dancers stand back to the pole, and the single performers do good regional steps opposite them, adding the clack of their castanets to the screech of the *Cobla*. Even then it is not finished, for the *dichos*, traditional verses, must be said, each man in turn addressing his girl. These are satirical, calling attention to the foibles of the village worthies, or to something laughable in a member of the audience. A Fool goes with the dancers, the Big Gipsy, lashing about him with a thong, and the men wear bells on their legs, while in one village, as in Cotswold Syresham, half the dancers, who are all men, are dressed in long white women's skirts. These costumes and characters take this Catalan Maypole right into the order of ceremonial dances, to which indeed it belongs, coming out at Carnival only and not in May. It is a stirring example of a Maypole rite, and with variants extends right down into Valencia, appearing also in Castile, Teneriffe and the Canary Islands. *Sellenger's Round* on moonshine nights about Maypoles becomes a simple enough affair compared with these.

CHAPTER VIII

HORNS, HOOFS AND FEATHERED FOWLS

Come in, come in, thou Hobby-horse,
And bring thy old Fool at thy arse.
Come in, come in, thou Dragon stout,
And take thy compass round about.
(*The Revesby Play*)

HERE we may exclaim with the Catalan Fool 'Nobody like us!' for it would be difficult indeed to find more extraordinary survivals than the men-beasts who still run and dance in old England, when seasonal obligations compel them to do so.

Out of time now and really belonging to the mid-winter festival, the Horn dancers of Abbots Bromley issue forth on the Monday after September 4th, a date ruled by the dedication of their church and co-inciding with their Wakes week. They find the horns hanging up in the church, and are sped on their dancing way by the Vicar from the church door, for they must carry 'the Luck' to the farthest farms, the most hidden cottages. Too late to see the start, we followed, and at midday met them. It will be impossible to forget the first sight of them down at the bottom of a deep lane, overhung by the great oaks of Bagot Park. They were moving up quietly and without talk, reds and greens showing faintly, what light there was catching tossing heads and sliding along great spreading antlers. Not our light fallow deer, but enormous heads they were, and seemed to fill the lane between the hedges. The cows in the fields on either side escorted them, tails up, wild eyes looking askance at reindeer in England. They turned into a farm gate, ranged themselves in single file, and with the buzz of their accordion began to circle the barton. There were six men-deer, each bearing his horns on a stick close to and as though springing from his head, one man-horse, a Fool, a hunter boy twanging a bow, a triangle boy, and a tall man-woman with a gentle, rustic face, the very Maid Marian we saw with the Morris, and actually calling herself so. The horse marks the time with snapping jaws, as the bow twangs and the accordion pumps out gay, common tunes. The circle becomes a serpentining line, the leader, followed by all, cuts between the second and third men, grunts a command not unlike the stag he is, at which they form two lines face to face, meet and retire, cross over and back. And that is all their dance is to-day, yet once they danced 'the Heys and Country dances'. The farmer and his wife bring out beer, the horns are piled on the ground, and every one takes a long pull and a moment's rest.

Their costumes have no tradition behind them. They were designed by the rather too knowledgeable wife of a former Vicar, and it is plain she took for her models the dresses of the Morris men, with the Fool, Hobby-horse and Maid Marian, depicted in the famous Betley window. I suspect the former man-woman, no doubt considered coarse by the helpful lady, assumed her name with Maid Marian's dress. But the Fool once had a furry cap to link him with a thousand other folk Fools, and the leadership has been in the same family for several hundred years, so they say—and such family traditions are found all over Europe and are not to be despised. Presently the weighty horns are once more raised, the reindeer men wind out of the barton, and away across the park-like meadows beneath the great oaks left behind by the receding forest. It all sounds quiet and rather dull perhaps, but you should see them dance into the village street once their day's round is finished.

'That's the time to see them,' says the policeman proudly. Like most folk festivals the evening ends with drinking, but by that time the horns are safely back in the care of the church.

The Hobby of Abbots Bromley is quite overshadowed by his more famous and rarer companion beasts, but other winter horses still trot out, and we will look at two of them, one in western Glamorganshire, the other in eastern Isle of Thanet. The first really leaves an uncomfortable impression of something 'not quite right', as people say, something rather dangerous, making one glad to hear the familiar church bell, to see friendly lights from low cottage windows. A frightful object is in the dark street, catching gleams of light on grinning skulls' teeth, showing flashes of white as it rises and falls in awful rearing movements. To add to the horror, as it approaches, people rush to their doors to slam them, and one hears bolts drawn inside. However, if one sticks to one's ground with a firm exterior, the awesome object resolves itself into a horse's skull decorated with bits of ribbon and finery, a white sheet hanging from its neck and enwrapping the stick and the person who carries it. A description from the *Gentleman's Magazine* of 1842 uses almost the same words. 'I saw . . . in the doorway, with the outline well defined in the moonlight, erect, a great white Horse, furiously tossing his head about.'

And so he has done for many a year before that, and ever since, but the bearer is now a boy, so the rearing ghost Horse is shorter than the one the 'Gentleman' saw, and thank heaven for it. When men carried it about they had a verse improvisation contest with the people behind the door, and if these won the Horse had to move off defeated, but if, as usually happened, the Horse company won, the door was opened and drinks and money given. The strangest thing about the ghost Horse is his name, *Mari Lwyd* (Holy Mary). One can indeed imagine the Virgin invoked at such a sight, but how came her name to be applied to the creature itself? Far from holy he must be of pagan, and exceedingly obstinate pagan, extraction.

The Isle of Thanet Horse is less realistic, for his head is a wooden and painted one, but his jaw opens and shuts rather horribly, and he is made in precisely the same way as his holy Welsh brother, a falling sheet wrapping the bearer, whose legs show below. A Wagoner shouts and cracks his whip, and Mollie sweeps the ground about them, for here again, without Morris or Sword dancers, is the ubiquitous man-woman, dancing in the usual gravely comic style, and even standing on her head.

The Hooden Horse of Kent cannot compare, however, with Padstow's Old Hoss, for whom the scene now shifts to a Cornish fishing town, the season the last night of April, every door open, the streets full of men, excitement in the air. The magic-making moment has come and the excitement centres round the 'Golden Lion', for in its stable lies a shadowy creature, awaiting, as he has waited through twelve long months, the day of his triumph. Midnight strikes, and voices go shouting through the night, witnessing that he has come to life again.

> 'Rise up, Mrs. Johnston, we wish you well and fine,
> (For Summer is a-come unto day).
> The horse is in his stable and is waiting for a ride,
> In the merry morning of May.'

The first perambulation of the town has begun. Verses suitable to the people within are sung beneath the windows, a pretty girl gets a compliment, the rich man of Padstow hears

> 'Rise up, Mr. Rosevear, we wish you well and fine,
> (For Summer is a-come unto day).
> You've a shilling in your pocket and I wish it was in mine,
> In the merry morning of May.'

It is not till next morning's procession that we can examine the creature properly. By the light of a May day what a terrific object he is. His once horse-shape is now circular, he is a good five feet in diameter and as black as the devil. He seems to be a round, walking dinner-table, its heavy cloth falling to the floor. From the table's rim protrudes a wooden horse-head with a wavy beard made of a cow's tail. But the really terrifying part of him is the locomotive power which rises from the middle of the dinner-table. The man inside wears a 'hood', which mask is three feet high, topped with a horse-tail plume, and furnished with two glaring eyes, white rimmed and paralysing, while out of a ravenous mouth hangs a broad red tongue. Above this horse-face are the letters O.B. painted in white. These, I am assured, initial 'Old Hobby'.

Certainly neither the British Isles nor any other country can produce anything stranger or more purely diabolic than Padstow's Old Hoss. He is stupendous, amazing, terrifying. He comes, not from the freedom of prehistory, but rather from the terrors of the Dark Ages. If Padstow were in Spain he might have been born of the Inquisition. How far removed is he from his boat-shaped brother of Minehead, from the elegantly soaring Horses of Languedoc, and from that comfortable, homely little animal which trots out at Glarus in Switzerland. Perhaps special circumstances gave rise to his conception in Cornish Celtic minds, or is it the result of the absolute merging of man into horse? There is no question of horse and rider, the black terror is entirely animal. This actual horse has been stabled at the 'Golden Lion' since the days of the Spanish Armada, according to the licensee. The cloth is tarpaulin and the wood thick with the paint of years. If one could scrape off each annual coat one might arrive at the creature's age, but even so he had predecessors. He frightened off a French raiding-party once, which is not surprising, for by his mere appearance he, like Sir Nicholas Pelham, did repel 'em back aboard, but his heyday probably began before Stonehenge was built. What he did then that he does now—at least as well as he can, taking policemen and such moderns into account. All day long the May Carol sounds in the streets,

> 'Unite, unite, we'll all unite,
> For Summer is a-come unto day,'

varied from time to time by the Day Song, dirge-like, and somewhat archaic both in words and music, except for a reference to those 'French dogs' of the raid. Like the Carol quoted in the Maypole section it tells plainly what they are at.

> For we are to fetch home the Summer and the May O,
> For Summer is i-come O
> And Win-i-ter is agone O!

They, like the people the Puritans so hated, are magicking in the spring. From time to time the horse sinks to the ground—can you picture that black bulk spread on the cobble-stones? Then his attendant the 'Teazer' or 'Clubman' gives him a stinging blow with the club he carries, and up rises the Hoss imbued with new life, gambols heavily down the street, while the girls run screaming, for fear of being caught beneath the 'cloak'. The latter used to be besmeared inside, as were also his hands, with black lead which left its mark on his victims. But this is another sign-manual of a Nature fertility rite, and still another, if one be yet needed, is the Maypole set up in the town, and decorated with fresh greenery picked that morning at dawn.

Off they used to go to Treator Pool, where the Hoss had to drink and the bystanders be sprinkled, for if you make artificial rain Nature will follow suit according to the laws of sympathetic magic, and she has never yet failed in the west country. So from morning till night the annual rite is worked out, every one wearing a nosegay, every one eating and drinking a great deal, especially the latter.

'The only day in the year that we does what we likes,' says 'Signor Brentano' of the accordion.

'You caan't do 'un on tea-water,' says the hooded

THE HOBBY-HORSE AT ATHENS
(*above*)

AND AT PADSTOW, CORNWALL
(*below*)

occupant of the Hoss in muffled tones. All the old Mayers are of that opinion, and the 'Sailor' naturally feels the need of liquid refreshment, so most of them think but poorly of 'them Temperance people' and their upstart, rival horse.

We may not think much of 'them foreign 'arses' either, but a few must be exhibited all the same, and after a glance they can, like the young lady at the ball, be trotted back again. A whole bevy of them until just lately came out at Fréjus, in Provence, on the day of St. François de Paul. They were led by one bigger one, danced to church, where they were accommodated with seats on the steps of the altar, and there they all sat decorously during mass. France is peculiarly rich in these animals, and one of the most interesting is the *Chevalet* of Ste. Lumine de Contais, who on Whit Sunday goes to mass like those of Fréjus, and who afterwards, with two attendant swordsmen, dances round an oak said to have been planted especially for his convenience. One of the biggest is the *Poulain* of Pezenas, celebrated since 1226, and so enormous a colt that he needs several men beneath his cloth, yet manages to dance after his *donneur d'avoine*; and the smallest and most agile is certainly the Basque *Zamalzain* who will perform his *entrechats huit* in another chapter.

While *en route* for the *Mulaferas* of Catalonia let us just mention the *Tarasque* of Tartarin's Tarascon, for these first astonishing creatures are sometimes Wild Mules as their name betokens, sometimes as much a Dragon as the *Tarasque* himself. Down in the Penedès district, south of Barcelona, lives a splendid Dragon, quite new and spruce, with bat-like wings, and a curled, barbed tail all green and shiny, for like our Mummers' defunct Dragon

> His head is made of iron,
> His body is made of steel.

The creature we have come to see, however, belongs to the Catalan Pyrenees, and at Berga comes rolling out in the Corpus Christi procession. At the town *festa* a few days later he will be out again, after a fight between Hobby-horses and Moors. These Hobbies are conventional and seem to be there merely for the sake of their riders, and one wonders why real horses cannot be used for so stiff and stylized a battle-dance, but the *Mulafera* is quite another question. He is of the Padstow Hoss type, though larger and yet more bulky. One would judge him an elephant rather than an equine animal, but for his outrageous length of neck, and his disagreeable habit of putting his head on to balconies and into windows to belch out fire and smoke. Such behaviour rules him out of the Wild Mule class and puts him right into the Dragon category, so he may be labelled a hybrid, and leaves the impression that the *Tarascs, Drags* and Mules of Catalonia have not an altogether clean pedigree sheet. His fire-raising is accompanied by rolls on the biggest drum you ever saw, and men and boys clamber up everywhere possible for the pleasure of receiving a mighty hiccup of smoke in their faces. When his stock of squibs has all been thus blown out of his mouth, he retires vaingloriously, and leans his chin upon a wall, while devils fight St. Michael and a little attendant angel, before yet another creature takes the floor. This time it is a feathered fowl of prodigious size, an Eagle on a pair of human legs. He wears a crown upon his royal bird's head, and when the *Cobla* band begins to play *l'Aliga* begins to dance. He manages well and elegantly, his Catalan legs in smartly cross-gartered *alpargatas* (the string-soled shoes of the country), stepping neatly, with excellently pointed toes. His finale allows his natural instincts scope, though he preys with his tail instead of with his beak. The male portion of the crowd, not yet satiated by the Dragon's fiery breath, follow the Eagle as he circles the square, first at a respectful distance, then closing in, so that as his pirouettes get up speed they may crouch and let the gigantic tail swirl over them. If they misjudge their moment, so much the worse for them. They say this is the Eagle of St. John the Evangelist, and it is true that it has appeared in ecclesiastical processions since the fifteenth century. It may quite probably have come from an interlude devised by the Church to amuse and instruct the common folk, but for the origins of the Wild Mule we must look beyond medieval Corpus Christi inventions, and link him with his fellows of Padstow and Pezenas who owe no Christian allegiance whatsoever.

The organizers of these processions were forced to admit many strange characters into their ranks—presently we shall find dancers there, leaping and jingling—so if Galician and Portuguese Dragons, crunching little boys and shouting obscene jokes to the crowd, may escort the most sacred of all Church perambulations, why not the more seemly Wild Mule? Reforms in the Church took less effect in Spain than in any other Roman Catholic country, chiefly owing to the traditionalism of Charles-Quint and the awe he inspired in the Vatican as elsewhere, so even had they so wished (and it is certain they did not), no purifying local authorities ever dared do as did the Mayor of Chester in 1599. Being 'a godly and zealous man', he took upon himself to break up the civic monsters, four giants, one unicorn, one dragon, one dromedary, one camel and six hobby-horses, so that they 'could not goe'.

The scene now shifts again, this time to eastern Europe, and here come Roumanian Hobby-horses, who never attempted lining up in Church processions, so frankly pagan are they. They are connected with both All Souls' Day and with the Midwinter feasts according to their district. The former compose a brotherhood, and each member undergoes an initiation ceremony before he may take part. They gather at cross-roads or where nine boundaries meet; their leader ties bells upon their legs and sprinkles them with water nine times. They carry with them a decorated stick, a kind of Maypole with ribbons, adding wormwood and garlic to keep away evil influences. At the end of their nine days' dancing—the reiterated period of nine, a magic number, is worth attention—this pole is thrown into the river. They consist of an uneven number of dancers, a Dumb Dancer who is the Fool, masked and lashing a whip, and yet another man disguised as a goat. During the proceedings one of them dies, is loudly lamented, and comes to life again. Here we recognize the central motif of our own Mummers' play, while to make these Roumanian brothers yet more mysterious we learn that in the eighteenth century they dressed as women, wore crowns of leaves and flowers, and assumed high, feminine voices.

The Roumanian *Calusar* is geographically, and perhaps also culturally, a half-way house between Polish and Greek examples of the Hobby-horse. The *Konik Zwierzyniecki*, a bearded horseman in a conical Tartar hat, astride a most imposing Hobby, figures in the procession held on the octave of Corpus Christi at Cracow. Legend links him with a victory over invading Cossacks in the thirteenth century. True or false—and the tale seems to repeat the exploit of the Padstow Hoss—there is no such legend to account for the monster I saw in Greece one clear February morning at Carnival time. It was on the outskirts of Athens, of all unpromising places. The thin skirl of a pipe caught my ear, and rounding a corner I came upon a magnificent 'Hoss' festooned all over with paper streamers, baleful of eye, and with a miniature Greek flag stuck jauntily behind its ear. The 'rider' was an Attic peasant in characteristic black cap, sleeveless waistcoat, and billowing white *foustanella*, complete with the most ingeniously deceptive false legs hung on either side, while his own were hidden from sight. He had two attendants, one to pipe to him, the other, more prosaically, to pass round the hat. To a queer little oriental tune he began to dance, prancing and curvetting in the best equine style, swinging first to the left and then to the right, and bucking like any broncho. Long after he had disappeared from sight I could still hear the pipe in the distance, urgent as the pipes of Pan himself, proclaiming Spring and the rebirth of all things living.

CHAPTER IX

RELIGIOUS DANCES

To-morrow shall be my dancing day.
(*Cornish Carol*)

MANY of our British folk-festivals have succeeded in living on free from Church interference. Our Beltane fires, for instance, have not been harnessed to St. John the Baptist as they have been almost everywhere on the Continent, and midwinter fire-festivals such as the 'Burning of the Clavie' at Burghead have never received so much as a Christian veneer. While our Maypoles and Morris men were for some long time enclosed within the ecclesiastical fold our Sword dancers and Mummers remained outside it. Other guisings were taken in and then expelled again, as at Perth where eight men confessed that they were Corpus Christi players and promised never to 'mell' with such things again.

At a very early date the Church adopted Well Dressing and Rogation Processions, both of which were pre-Christian in origin and show it in spite of centuries of discipline. Well Dressers not only sang hymns but danced in procession, and of the Rogation perambulations feasting formed an important part. One year the processionists of St. Margaret's, Westminster, consumed fish, butter, cream, milk and conger eels. The Gospel was read in the corn-fields, and boys were whipped on the Parish boundaries just as the 'bounds' are beaten to-day. The Puritans were not slow to condemn in these customs 'idolatries maintained by the Church of England', one ironically asking in 1554 whether the corn understood what was read to it on gang days, and another in 1602 inquiring whether the clergy 'patiently winked at any rytes wherein hath been apparent superstition, as gadding and raunging about with procession'.

In those days dancing in the churches was quite common, the Morris was admitted, and down to the nineteenth century the villagers of Batford and Wishford had the right to dance in Salisbury Cathedral. The apprentices of York claimed a similar right in the Minster on Shrove Tuesday of all unhallowed occasions, and even to-day the Castleton Garland dance is quite under the wing of the Church, for the ringers meet in the belfry to organize it, the Queen's horse is led by the Parish Clerk (if there still is one), the Church pays for the rod on which the Garland is hung, the latter is hoisted from off the King's head on to the church tower and kept there, and the proceedings begin with a visit to the Vicar.

To see dancing in sacred precincts to-day, however, one must cross the Channel and travel to more southern climes.

It was the day of Corpus Christi, a brilliant, sunny afternoon in late May. In the largest Gothic cathedral in all Christendom the sun's radiance was softened, and the lighted candles before the altar cast a mysterious golden gloom into the farther recesses. Golden, too, was the gilt railing round the chancel, and golden the great reredos. The service was drawing to a close, and the congregation, men in dark clothes and women in black mantillas and high combs, were beginning to shift impatiently in their seats. Presently, it came to an end, and a procession of priests and acolytes emerged from the enclosed choir and moved across to the chancel with many genuflexions and much swinging of censers. While the choir sang the solemn *Tantum Ergo,* a little band of musicians established themselves to one side, close under the altar.

Now the singing ceased and the *Seises* appeared, the famous dancing boys of Seville Cathedral, whose performance attracts visitors from far and wide.

There were ten of them, about twelve years of age. They were dressed like pages in a Velazquez picture, in striped doublets and white knee-breeches. The red and yellow of their doublets was echoed in the laces of their white shoes and in the tassel at the end of the white sash flung over the right shoulder. They carried beribboned castanets and seventeenth-century plumed hats tucked under their arms.

Lining up, they fell on their knees before the altar, asking permission of the Chapter to begin. Then, in the middle of the chancel, they formed up in two lines, the orchestra struck up and the dance began. Putting on their plumed hats, and singing as they went, they moved with grave, unhurried dignity forwards, backwards or sideways, the double line constantly meeting, retreating, crossing, dissolving and reforming again at right angles. Sometime their nasal chanting would cease and be replaced by the rhythmic clicking of their castanets. Once or more they formed a circle and entwined in the stateliest of Heys.

There were ten figures in all, but it was neither in these nor in the steps that the fascination of the performance lay. Here, in a great cathedral, in a crowded city, was still being enacted in the twentieth century that most ancient of all traditions, the sacred dance. We had stepped out of the New Testament straight back into the Old.

The *Dance of the Seises* is first mentioned in writing in 1508, but it must actually be far older. It used to be done not only in Seville but also in Toledo, and probably in other less important places. When dancing fell into disfavour in the Church it owed its survival to a fortunate chance. In 1685 a Spanish prelate, Jaime Palafox y Cardona, was consecrated Bishop of Seville. Forthwith he decided that the *Dance of the Seises* was unseemly and must be suppressed. The Chapter stood up for their privileges and appealed to the Pope. For seventeen years the question remained in suspense. Then, according to current tradition, judgement was pronounced. The dance might continue, but only so long as the boys' clothes lasted. When they wore out it must cease. They have never yet worn out and never will, not by any miracle, but by the simple expedient of repairing them again and again so that the original fabric has been replaced many times over, but never all at once. They may look like new to-day, but the judgement has been honoured in the letter if not in the spirit, and the dance continues.

When Blanco White wrote his *Letters from Spain* just over a hundred years ago, not only was the *Dance of the Seises* done inside the Cathedral, but the procession of Corpus Christi included no less than three other sets of dancers, a Sword dance, a *Chacona*

(Chaconne) and a group called *Valencianos*. There were also seven 'Giants', dressed to display next year's fashions, who danced just as the giants still dance in the Cathedral at Santiago de Compostella on St. James's Day. Of these Galician giants some represent Moors, and two are fat and comic, one in a yachting cap and the other dressed as a woman. As mass ends they enter the nave, and the clergy leave hurriedly, as though in tacit disapproval.

The attitude of the Church towards religious dances has been curiously inconsistent and apparently haphazard. On the whole it has been disapproving, although many interesting performances have contrived to slip through the sieve of its disapproval and others have revived after many years when the ban against them had been forgotten. The pretext for ecclesiastical disapprobation has varied with the occasion. Thus, in Germany, the Sword dances of the Guilds were attacked by the Catholic clergy on the ground that they were pagan in character, and by the Lutherans on the ground that they savoured of Popery. Elsewhere, the excuse (and it may have been more than an excuse) for their prohibition was the disorders and brawls which these dances so often seem to have occasioned. As early as 1486 a municipal decree of the city of Vittoria in northern Spain records the 'fine of sixty maravedis incurred by those who performed Sword dances, owing to the disturbances and bloodshed which they caused'.

Histories of the dance generally quote the *Dance of the Seises* as the only surviving example of the religious dance, but this is far from being the case. You may find it in no other great cathedral, but there are many places both in Spain and Portugal where the young men still dance in processions and even in church, and who shall say that they do not find favour in the eyes of the Lord?

In 1932, at Braga in north Portugal, once the primatial city of all the Spains, we witnessed a performance as remarkable if not quite as elaborate as the *Dance of the Seises*, the *Dance of King David*. This dance forms part of the procession of St. John's Day in which it is preceded by the *Shepherd's Cart*, which resembles nothing so much as one of the medieval Chester cart-plays. The 'cart' was a big lorry, drawn by oxen and garlanded with greenery, on which was erected a large and unsubstantial stage rock. Half-way up stood a small boy representing St. John, dressed in silks and velvets with periwig and painted face, and leading a live lamb adorned with red ribbon. The presence of the lamb seems to have suggested Shepherds and Shepherdesses, and here they were, a group of overdressed children. Every now and again the lorry paused, and a child angel shot up from inside the rock, his feet resting unsteadily on a piece of woolly cloud, and screeched a Gounod-like hymn. At this signal the Shepherds and Shepherdesses went through some simple Country dance figures, and this pocket 'Mystery' came to an end.

Next came King David and his courtiers. They were dressed in the sort of costume the seventeenth century imagined to be oriental. Their coats were of velvet, the trimming divided into squares by silver braid. Their would-be turbans had high crowns, they wore lace frills round their necks, knee-breeches, pink stockings and curious white boots with a ruche of silk turned over the ankle. Each of them carried a musical instrument, guitars, fiddles, flutes and even a 'cello. To do their dance they formed up in a semi-circle. Two 'Princes' now danced out with a much employed English Morris step, bowed to the King and retired to their places. Out came King David himself and imitated them exactly. Then the semi-circle divided into two files, one on either side of him, and executed a march in two concentric circles, one moving clockwise and the other 'widdershins'.

The whole was orderly and well-rehearsed. The King especially showed great earnestness, wearing the expression of gravity common to folk-performers and singers, and reminding me in far-off Braga of a team of Devon step-dancers competing on a cart.

The Kingship, like the leadership of the Abbots Bromley Horn Dancers, is hereditary, the father of the present holder having been in office many years.

I believe the *Dance of King David* to be a priest-handled Morris. 'King David danced before the Ark.' It is so easy an explanation and so biblical an excuse for these disreputable old customs, and I have heard it from priests of many different tongues. The dance is not mentioned under its present name until 1726, but long before that Braga possessed a *Mourisca*, which came out on the Day of St. John with a King and all proper appurtenances.

As late as 1875 the little Portuguese town of Pedrogão Pequeno preserved a *Mourisca*, the description of which puts us very much in mind of the *Dance of King David*. This, too, belonged to St. John's Day. There were seven men in skirts with entwined ribbons, jackets and conical caps with flowers. As at Braga, they played instruments as they danced, the last couple carrying wands (which may well once have been swords) with large bunches of carnations on the top end. The King wore a shawl and a crown, and carried a sword and a shield on which St. John's lamb was painted. They first advanced with majestic steps to the altar of the chapel and bowed before the Saint. The dance lasted half an hour and 'much resembled French *contre-danses*'. I have no doubt that by the end of the nineteenth century it did, and to make quite sure that the old spirit was exorcized they concluded with a genuflexion to the Saint. The King, however, retained sufficient activity to make a pirouette on the left foot, at which signal all cried loudly, 'Long live my companion, St. John the Baptist!'

If in Germany some of the evidence goes to suggest that the Sword dance was a product of the Guilds, all the evidence in the Iberian Peninsula points the other way. The Sword dances described in an earlier chapter are linked with religion, if only by the fact that they are performed on the principal festivals of the ecclesiastical calendar. In many of them, however, the link is much closer, and this indeed is as it should be. 'The Sword dance', wrote Larramendi in the middle of the eighteenth century, 'is for grave occasions such as Corpus Christi processions. The dancers enter in silence without shouting or noise other than their music; nor do women take part in the dance, nor any other thing which might make it less worthy of the Church or of the presence of the Lord.' This might be a description of the scene to-day when, on July 2nd, the Sword dancers of Zumarraga do their dance before the altar in the church of Santa Maria la Antigua.

It is curious how the festival of Corpus Christi (which the Basques call Phesta Berri, the 'new feast', presumably because it was established as recently as

1246) seems to have been particularly associated with the Sword dance. This festival forms a link between the Church and Guilds, for all over Europe the Guilds were responsible for furnishing and equipping the various features of the procession on this day. At Oñate, no distance from Zumarraga, a Sword dance by skirted dancers is a feature of the Corpus Christi procession. They dance with castanets in their hands before the Priest bearing the Host, while the Archangel Michael struts magnificently, armour gleaming, plumes waving, little wings fluttering, and the twelve Apostles march six on either side of him. The following Sunday and its octave are the occasion in the French Basque province of Basse-Navarre of a striking survival of the religious dance. If you take a drive, through the region of Arbéroue on these two Sundays, you may see a sight, naïve, touching, slightly comic, certainly never to be forgotten. Down a honeysuckle lane between hay-fields comes a procession so bedecked with ribbons, white clothes, mirrors, immense busbies, that you wonder whether every one has not gone mad. This 'Regiment', as it is called, is led by a band, the drums beating in the inflammatory way that Basque drums have. At its head come the *Sapeurs*, at its tail the *Voltigeurs*, four boys who dance even more madly than the rest. They all dance into church, they line the aisle, the *Sapeurs* mount the steps to the raised sanctuary.

There they remain throughout mass, and at the elevation, instead of falling on their knees, the Regiment will dance, each man in his place, thudding the stocks of their rifles on the floor. At this moment a *Sapeur* has even been known to leap on to the altar itself.

Once again, through Pyrenean passes, we cross the border. The frontier-post with grand simplicity says: Navarra. It is a day of stormy skies and brilliant stormy green, of hidden mountain-tops and drenched slopes, the bracken bowed down and silvery wet. The frontier river, the Bidassoa of Peninsular War fame, is in spate, as brown as Spanish chocolate. The side valley to the south is of a green still more intense, like the green of Mauresque lustre ware. A vast church presides over the village of Lesaca, which can still show you the house where the Duke of Wellington made his headquarters. Bells in the open belfry turn right over as they boom out the hour of mass. It is the day of the patronal festival, and the patron is the Saint and Bishop, Fermin. On this same day in Pamplona, the capital of the province, bulls are being killed, and a little Hobby-horse prances and curvets about. But here, enclosed within a wall of sombre mountains, girls in black mantillas and men in short black smocks make their way churchwards.

Inside the church the gilt of a huge reredos

gleams in the darkness, the altar candles burn with a different coloured gold, and over the entire floor of the great chairless nave the colour is repeated. Little flames burn low on the ground in front of each shrouded figure, and are dimly reflected in the polished floor. A sonorous organ, played by some master hand, leads the singing of a sixteenth-century mass. Its rolling mode time and again resolves into a satisfying tierce in Picardy. Incensed twilight diapered with tiny flames, threaded with gilt, filled with splendid tone.

Across this strikes a shrill music, an ardent, excited drumming. The doors fling open, and out sways St. Fermin on the shoulders of his sons for his yearly perambulation. He is met at the doorway by a great undulating flag, curling, dipping, bowing to him. Now there come a group of white-clad, scarlet-béreted youths, jingling bell-pads on their shins. Ribbons, crossed on their chests, pass beneath breast and back plates composed of sacred pictures, crosses and symbols worked in sequins. The swords of these Sword dancers have dwindled into sticks round which red ribbons twine pacifically.

There are two rows of six, the thirteenth, the Captain, carrying no ' sword '. At the sound of the *txistu* pipes he dashes forward, and face to face with his Patron Saint he dances out his heart and soul. His feet alternately fly above his head, sideways he goes and back again, then shoots straight up into the air in a final *entrechat.* Panting, satisfied that his yearly devotion is duly paid, he picks up the points of the sticks held by his first two men and leads out the double file locked hilt and point, himself the apex of the long procession. Every now and again he turns back, raises his arms, and each file performs a single-under, one on each side of their Captain.

The black-clad men of the parish process in pairs separated by the whole breadth of the street. The musicians march in the middle, the dancers work their way from the head of the procession to their post below St. Fermin's swaying golden figure and back again. The women, apart as always in the Basque country, modestly bring up the rear. When the Saint is safely housed for another year, the step becomes a quick march. The company briskly passes to another street, down the middle of which runs a brook. The gaily bound sticks are lifted, meet to form an arch, and beneath the arch march the Mayor, the Council and the Priest. Now the Captain goes to the centre of the little bridge. Six of his men leap upon the wall on one side of the stream, six upon the other. There, like great white-plumed birds, aligned on a perch, with pink and glittering breasts, they break out into their best steps, the Captain on the bridge always out-dancing his men. All finish with their famous *entrechats* upon the narrow wall.

It is only a statue of St. Fermin which is carried round at Lesaca. At Lequeitio on the Biscayan coast, another Saint, St. Peter this time, is represented on his day by a living man who himself does the dancing. Every year on June 29th the members of the Fishermen's Guild elect their officers for the coming year, and carry round the town a big wooden chest containing their archives. This used in bygone days to be surmounted by a statue of St. Peter, escorted by two companions of the Guild representing St. John and St. Andrew. The statue used to be taken down to the sea and beaten as an earnest of what the Saint might expect should he fail to provide good catches of fish. Then the Church stepped in to prohibit this manifest disrespect to the Saint, and replaced him by a dancer wearing, of all incongruous things, a top hat, and carrying a banner worked with St. Peter's keys to denote his origin. Balanced precariously on his stand, he is carried through the streets by the officers of the Guild, and dances before the houses of the Mayor and notables of the little town. More fortunate than his apostolic predecessor, he escapes a thrashing.

Farther to the west in the Montaña de Santander, where the Picos de Europa tower up into the sky whiter than the piled-up cumulus clouds behind them, a statue of St. Peter is still borne in procession on his day at Comillas, on the coast. Before it a long procession of white-clad young men is dancing backwards, two by two, called *picayos*. They dance, not with swords or sticks, but with beribboned castanets and fluttering streamers. On either side of the pathway pace the *pandereteras*, girls in regional dress, playing large and sonorous tambourines with fingers as agile as the feet of the men. Do not imagine the *pandereta* can be played by banging it with the knuckles and rattling its bells. It is as hard to play properly as the castanets, the fingers being used in a peculiar sliding movement difficult to acquire.

The *picayos* are not peculiar to Comillas. They may be seen dancing before the statue of Our Lady at the fishing village of San Vicente de la Barquera, or before the Virgin of the Fields at Cabezón de la Sal on August 12th. What is peculiar to Comillas is the 'old woman's dance', to which dancers and singers turn their attention when, the ancient image safe home again, they have closed their act of adoration with a triple genuflexion.

A row of old village dames draped in their best headkerchiefs and Manilla shawls are sitting in a row in the little *plaza*. They are tambourining vigorously, and singing, too, in their feeble old voices, but they keep a lively eye on the *picayos* who now approach. One, clacking his castanets, lightly bounding, presents himself before the old lady of his choice, who coolly remains seated and will not stir till her young gallant kneels before her. Up she then gets, and, more elegantly by far than her grand-daughter, begins to step to and fro, her gentle, low, light steps contrasting finely with the leaps and twirls of her partner. Presently all the old ladies, having been sought out as partners, are up and at it, and a very pretty compliment it is, for they are the repositories of traditional verse and tune, and the best *pandereteras* in the place.

The religious dances which we have described are all from south-west Europe, but this little corner of our continent is not the only place where the sacred dance still serves a sacred object. There is the celebrated dance to the shrine of St. Willibrod at Echternach in Luxemburg, which, more than a dancing procession, is a dancing pilgrimage in which not only a band of picked young men as we have hitherto seen, but every single pilgrim dances. They come pouring in from the surrounding villages, even from the distant German town of Prüm, and these must set out on Whit Tuesday to reach the shrine at the right time next day.

The pilgrims are led by their parish priests who tramp, fully robed, beside the panting files. A cloud of dust hangs over their road as over moving herds.

Until the seventeenth century only men danced, but now women have pushed their way into the ranks and step it as valiantly as their husbands and sons. As many as 14,000 people may be on the roads, and they must start early, for they cover their route twice over in their strange, traditional step, one back and two forward, which is hardly a 'best foot foremost'.

The place to choose for a first sight of them is on the high ground round the church. In they come, led now by the clergy and choir of Echternach who have been out to meet them, first crowds and crowds of men drawn up roughly four abreast, linked together with handkerchiefs or sticks to keep their formation, coats and waistcoats long since thrown off, broad Teutonic and flat frontier faces streaming with all-day sweat, tousled hair standing up on bullet heads. One lost count, and still they came, filling the street from end to end and from side to side, police pushing back the onlookers to keep a space clear.

As they drew nearer, the famous one step back and two forward began to give place to something even more exhausting and therefore more meritorious. One forward, one back, and now the ranks rise unsteadily and unevenly into the air, as every pilgrim jumps three times. Far down the street women's heads come into view, and here they are, keeping the same ranks, doing the same step, jumping the same weary jumps, all neatly dressed, but poor tired faces glistening and hair flying in the wind. Slowly and with difficulty, one forward, one back and three painful jumps, they crowd up the steps into the churchyard, some making for a great stone cross, others disappearing into the grateful dark of the building.

What do they do it for? Why step and jump for long hours under a broiling sun? Why cover long miles of stony, dusty road in the guise of dancing dervishes? They reply simply: 'In honour of our St. Willibrod who cures calves of St. Vitus' dance.'

One even stranger spectacle did the search for religious dances bring me, and this took me to windy Jaca on its high terrace, its back to the snowy Colorado, scene of one of the most tragic episodes of recent Spanish history. On the 25th of June the town celebrates its feast in honour of Santa Orosia, Christian saint and local thaumaturgical goddess. That is the moment to see Jaca casting off its rather red modernity and behaving as it did before its seventeen towers came down, and its encircling walls were laid flat.

When her head was still on her shoulders, Santa Orosia was a Czech missionary lady, probably Moravian, since Moravia is famous for its zeal, who came to Aragon to convert the heathen in the eighth century. Here, runs the legend, she was put to death by the Moors on the summit of the mountain behind Yebra de Basa. Miraculously a pious shepherd was directed first to where her body lay, and then to the severed head, taking the former to Jaca and retaining the latter in his own village of Yebra. There they remain to this day. On the 25th of June, the Bishop of the diocese comes up with his chaplains, accompanied by hordes of *endemoniados* (epileptics) who hope to be dispossessed of their devils by the wonder-working Saint. They go to her body to be cured if they live on the west of the Gallego river, to the head if to the east, and pilgrims and parish crosses follow the same rule.

Traditionally they should be met on the afternoon of June 29th by the ceremonial dancers of Jaca who perform their *Paleotada* (stick dance) before them into the town. They should then spend the night in vigil in the Cathedral. In 1933 neither tradition was observed, but on the 25th the procession was held as usual, the epileptics crowding round while the priests divested the body of the Saint of its coverings. Their hysteria increased as, one after another, the brocades and velvets, lavishly embroidered by devotees, were removed, and when at last the relic was revealed in all its desiccated and repulsive nakedness, a woman's strident voice culminated in a final shriek, 'Santa Orosia-a-a-a', while her guardians held her writhing body to the ground.

High on the mountain next day a different wind was blowing. Yebra keeps the feast on the 25th on the plateau above, and on the 26th in the village. Fresh air and an arduous climb put a different complexion on the proceedings. The parish priest steps out courageously, the small reliquary containing the Saint's head being borne by mountain stalwarts, and this time the dancers are not lacking to decorate the procession. Very early they all string into single file on the winding path, and begin the long rough climb to the Sanctuary. The dancers are spotlessly clean in their regional costume, over which are worn the sashes, ribbons, scarves and bells which turn them into members of the great European ritual brotherhood. Their hats have tall sprays of flowers, the leader flashes a mirror on his, while a cloud of ribbons floats down his back. In either hand they hold a stick, and before them marches their musician with his stringed drum and three-holed pipe. At the Sanctuary, the *Señor Cura* opens the reliquary and displays the head, and the *Paleotada* is danced. The whole day they all stay up there, eating and drinking, dancing and singing. Girls spread clean napkins on the turf, and out come wine-bottles and leathern wine-sacks, from which the men pour red jets down their parched throats. Casting off their hierophancy, the ritual dancers are lost in the crowd, make love, sing *Jotas*, and with difficulty are gathered together in the evening to return downhill in procession.

CHAPTER X

'A GREEN STAGE'

We are not the London actors
That act upon the stage;
We are the country people
That dances without wage.
(*Mummers' Play*)

IN the preceding chapters we have seen how closely the traditional dance is often bound up with drama. It is not impossible that all dancing is ultimately derived from pantomime, and that even those dances which we regard to-day as purely recreational have their remotest origin in mimic ceremonies performed for a serious purpose, and have only reached their present form through a long and gradual process of stylization. In this final chapter we will look at one or two of the more elaborate European festivals in which elements of dance, mime and drama are brought together, although we shall attempt no final assessment of the relation in which they stand to one another.

We saw that in England the Sword dances of the north country are accompanied by a play which is something more than a mere humorous or dramatic interpolation. We saw, too, that in southern England the play exists by itself, although there is reason to suppose that our Mummers once danced as well. The mumming-play unattended by dancing is, of course, no English monopoly, and is found all over Europe in a form which varies astonishingly little; astonishingly, that is to say, only if we are not prepared to admit that these are but particular and local variations on a general and ubiquitous theme.

In the island of Skyros in the Sporades, where Rupert Brooke lies buried, Mr. J. C. Lawson and Professor Dawkins have witnessed a very primitive Carnival dance. The principal characters are three in number: an Old Man, a Maid and a Frank. The Maid is a Man-Woman in bridal attire, the Frank has a sheep-bell tied to his waist and a conch-shell to blow, and the Old Man wears a shepherd's cloak inside out, a mask of animal skin or fur and fifty or sixty large sheep-bells fastened round his waist. There is little or no by-play, but a dance which may best be described in Mr. Lawson's words:

'The purpose of the leaping and dancing is solely to evoke as much noise as possible from the bell . . . the interior of a belfry with a peal being rung would be peace and quiet after the jar and jangle of hundreds of those goat-bells, when the troupe of dancers wheel suddenly round some corner and pour past down the rugged, slippery road, or at the end of the dance leap together into the air and come together with a crash which in those narrow alleys threatens to dislodge the very houses from the great rocky pinnacle to whose abrupt sides they cling.'[1]

A more developed mumming-play is reported from the village of Haghios Gheorghios in Thrace, where it is performed on Carnival Monday. The dramatis personae include two *Kalogheroi* with head-dress masks of animal-skin, blackened hands and the same sheep-bells round their waists, one carrying a cross-bow and the other a phallus; two 'Girls' or 'Brides', played of course by young men; an old woman carrying a basket containing a doll always referred to as a bastard; and a number of Gipsies and Policemen, the latter of whom appear to perform a sort of rudimentary Sword dance.

The drama is a complex and inconsequent affair, in which, among other things, a ploughshare is forged and a plough driven round widdershins, thus

[1] *Annual of the British School at Athens*, No. VI, p. 127.

linking the performance with regions so far apart as Germany, Lincolnshire, Catalonia and Portugal. The phallus-bearing *Kalogheros* becomes somehow identified with the bastard child, is married to one of the 'Girls', shot by his comrade, lamented by his wife, and comes to life again. In this instance he dispenses with the services of the usual Doctor, who, however, appears in similar mummings in Thessaly and Macedonia.

Similar doings in Roumania are, as we have seen, associated with the Hobby-horse dance, but it is in the wilder of the Alpine valleys that we must next seek this strange Carnival company with their still stranger ceremonies.

The *Achetringele* at Laupen in Switzerland on New Year's Eve brings out a horde of terrifyingly masked figures in skins with enormous cow-bells round their waists and long sticks in their hands, who rush wildly about, but neither dance nor act a play. They are clearly related to the Austrian *Perchtl* or *Perchten*, whose name is thought by some to be derived from the Saxon goddess Perachta, and by others from Claudia Procula, wife of Pontius Pilate, who besought her husband not to condemn Christ, and who, according to Tyrolese legend, was converted to Christianity after his death and made the Guardian Angel of the souls of unbaptized children. These Carnival 'runners' are found extensively in the provinces of Salzburg, Styria and the Tyrol, and are generally divided into two groups called respectively *schöne* (beautiful) and *schieche* (ugly) *Perchten* or sometimes *Faschinge*. The 'beautiful' ones are orderly in behaviour and handsomely dressed with little ribbons, bells and tall crowns, sometimes as much as four or five feet high, adorned with mirrors: the 'ugly' ones are of unruly demeanour and are clad in dirty rags, masked with the most grotesque and distorted faces and hung about with rats and mice, chains and cow-bells. All carry long sticks tipped respectively with ribbons or devils' heads. They seem to be well aware of their own unhallowed nature, for their tradition forbids them to pass a church, and enjoins them to hide like evil spirits when the church bells chime, a striking proof of their pre-Christian origin.

The Salzburg *Tresterer* whom I saw in 1934 were, practically speaking, dancing *Perchten*. They wore patterned cretonne shirts and shorts, beribboned socks, hats decorated with feathers and artificial flowers, and they carried handkerchiefs in their hands. They did a simple Round dance of Morris type, while their Fool, in a tall hat with an extending wooden trellis in his hand, skipped round the outside of the circle.

A Round dance is clearly an integral feature of these Shrovetide runnings, and we are indebted to

Mr. Rolf Gardiner for his kind permission to reproduce the following unpublished account of such a dance at the Styrian village of Krakau in 1928:

'All the while we could hear the bells approaching, and the intermittent cries of the bird-like voices. Then of a sudden, coming at right angles to our path, coming through the forest in a long single file, the procession appeared, running at a slow jog. The first a great tall fellow in a blood-red, tight-fitting costume, his height accentuated by a high-peaked fool's cap, rhythmically swinging a broom from side to side, driving away the evil spirits from the path of the spring. Behind him, another, completely covered in feathers, owls', hawks', starlings' feathers, and his head like a Viking's with two outspreading falcon wings. These precede the *Faschinge* (or Morris, as we should say), twelve youths in ceremonial white but with coloured kerchiefs and ribbons, and wearing high-peaked hats with "1928" stuck thereon in coloured paper and ribands streaming: in their hands, freshly cut wooden lances, twelve feet high, also flying streamers. They follow in single file, absorbed in their business. After them at a distance, four husbandmen similarly dressed in white smocks, but with snowdrops stuck in their curly hats, and great sonorous cow-bells dangling in their hands. Finally, in ragged disorder, a motley crew, mostly in tatterdamalion shirts and sooty faces. These now halloo and hail us and then promptly surround us, all talking at once. The sootiest face has a "horse" on a lead: at least there is a horse's head projecting out from a sort of wooden frame arrangement covered with sacking, the rump end being supported by a man-woman like the dirty Bet of the Yorkshire plays. The sooty face is trying to sell us the horse, and his garlicky breath and eager gestures persuade my companion all too easily. He grins, pays his two shillings and goes off with the horse. But, no! the horse must first be shod: and this is done most realistically by the sooty face and his minions, the final act being the shooting of a curious telescopic wooden trellis, at which the horse kicks nobly and champs the air like Bellerophon. The purchaser makes off again, the poorer by three shillings. But no!—once more ill luck pursues him; for after four yards with a groan and a jerk the horse collapses in the snow: such a forlorn collection of sacks, sticks, human legs and horse mask, strewn in fantastic disarray on the earth! Oh, dear! But now advance a doctor and his hussy. The doctor is as cocksure as all the mumming-play doctors in Europe. He has, of course, already saved the Republic from war, pestilence, famine and financial ruin: the Chancellor [Dr. Seipel] isn't even in the running! And now, just for one shilling, he'll reanimate that ramshackle heap on the ground! There's nothing else to do but to comply. And so the two of them bend down on either side of the poor beastie and prod its underparts, till with a wild snort and a kick, life is very much returned to its carcass.

'All this being done, the gang pick up their tackle and follow the now disappearing procession. They show no further interest in ourselves, although we meekly follow in their train. But look yonder! Outside the farmhouse they are doing the *Radl*, the Wheel dance. The four husbandmen stand two deep in a compact square ringing their bells vigorously to and fro. The tall, blood-red demon-driver leads his dancers round and round in a troy-town maze, like the last figure of *Bonnie Green Garters*. He has a quick, springy step, but his body is straight and poised, and he holds his broom, brush end upwards, balanced aloft. The others follow, intently, swerving round, with eyes unseeing or half closed and lances held upright in the right hand. It is an impressive dance, continuous and tense. But when the red-one has completed the serpentine twice to the centre and out again, he casts off with a sudden twist counter-clockwise, followed by the Feathers, and then by each single dancer at intervals, in turn, much in the same way as the dancers cast off from the hey in the Flamborough Sword dance. As each dancer completes his counter-clockwise twist, he leaps into the air, gives a bird-like whoop, and dashes away.'

The most elaborate of all these Austrian Carnival runnings is the *Schemenlaufen*, held every two or three years at the little town of Imst on the Inn above Innsbrück. As we saw in Chapter VI, Dr. Wolfram declares that it is the ritualistic festival of a secret society of men, and that 'the thousands of strangers who go . . . to watch this peculiar custom have no idea what they are really seeing'. *Schemen*, he explains, is an old Germanic word for 'ghost', and in his view all these 'runners' represent the 'Wild Hunt' of legend, the army of the dead.

Like so many Carnival festivities, the proceedings open in the morning with a procession satirizing the principal local events of the preceding year, called the *Figatter*. The true *Schemenlaufen* begins at noon. The *Schemen*, who are about twenty in number, are divided into two groups called *Scheller* and *Roller*, who are regarded not as 'beautiful' and 'ugly' like the *Perchten*, but as male and female, although needless to say they are all played by men. Their names relate to the bells they wear fastened to their broad leather belts, little sleigh-bells for the feminine *Roller* and huge cow-bells totalling as much as forty pounds in weight for the masculine *Scheller*. The difference between the sexes is indicated chiefly by their masks, smooth and chubby in the one case, boldly bearded and moustachioed in the other. Both alike wear Tyrolese leather breeches, scarves hanging from their heads and the *Schein*, a resplendent head-dress of flowers and fruit, arranged round a mirror. The *Scheller* carries a stick striped like a barber's pole, and the *Roller* a broom.

These handsome figures are parodied by so-called *Lagge Roller* and *Lagge Scheller*, whose ragged garments are adorned with pine-cones and wooden bells. Here, perhaps, may we find the equivalent of the 'ugly' *Perchten*. There are also a number of additional personages, notably *Sackner*, *Spritzer*, *Kübele Maien* and *Hexen*. The last named are witches, and a monstrous ill-favoured crew they are. Their masks are carved into deformed faces, covered with warts, the nose or chin ending in serpents' heads. They are presided over by a 'Witch Master' and a 'Witch Mother', and they have their own wild Round dance. To the other figures is confided the duty of clearing the way for the procession. The *Sackner*, who used to wear parti-coloured stockings like a Fool, strike the spectators with a sack filled with maize stalks, while the *Spritzer* squirt water in their faces and the *Kübele Maien* wet them with damp cloths. As in all these runnings the procession is the main thing, and the dance subsidiary to it.

It is a Round dance with much leaping into the air, such as will make the crops prosper, and there is actually a popular saying at Imst that the year in which the *Schemenlaufen* is held will always be a year of fruitfulness and prosperity.

By this time the reader will doubtless learn without surprise that to find anything so elaborate as these Austrian Carnival runnings he must go to the Pyrenees, and in particular to the Basque country. Let us then turn our backs on the maritime province of Labourd where Carnival brings out the queer Men-Women mentioned in Chapter V, and pass through Basse-Navarre where Giants and Wild Ladies dance attendance on the dramatic form here given to the 'rough music' which punishes such unseemly offences as the remarriage of a widow or widower or the beating of a husband by his wife.[1] This brings us to the highland province of Soule, where *Mascarades* are organized during the last weeks preceding Lent. This is no haphazard, fancy-dress masquerading such as takes place in Carnival in most southern countries, but an unbelievably complex performance governed by a strict tradition, which may be described as the grafting of a ballet on a mumming-play.

Mascarades (the word is always used in the plural)

[1] Cf. Violet Alford: French Basques: Cascarots and Cavalcades in *Music and Letters,* April 1929. Also Rodney Gallop: *A Book of the Basques,* 1930.

are carefully rehearsed from the New Year onwards, and at the appropriate season are invited to neighbouring villages, reserving their final performance for their own village on Shrove Tuesday, the last day of their existence. They march out in two companies known as the 'Reds' or 'Beautiful Ones' and the 'Blacks'. The finest dancers play the parts of the five principal 'Reds', that is to say, the *Zamalzain, Kantiniersa, Cherrero, Gatuzain* and *Enseñaria.* Except for the last, who is a Standard-Bearer, these correspond to our own Hobby-horse, Man-Woman, Sweeper and Fool. The 'hoss' is neither terrifying nor ridiculous but a magnificent young man wearing the dancers' dress of yellow breeches, scarlet tunic with breastplate of white sewn with gold studs and buttons, thick white stockings hand-knitted in openwork patterns, black velvet spats sewn with spangles, and white *espadrilles.* On his head is a high crown made of gold paper, ribbons, artificial flowers and little mirrors. The horse itself has a tiny head on a curved neck, an oblong frame through which the man stands, and a white lace flounce for a saddlecloth. The rider grasps his 'mount' by the neck and sways him up and down at every step. The white lace flounce billows round him like a ballet skirt, and the whole effect is light, graceful and extraordinarily exciting.

The *Kantiniersa* is a young man dressed in the

supposed costume of a French Army *cantinière*. He, too, wears the dancers' scarlet tunic, but shows his feminine character by a short blue skirt, little apron, and child's blue sailor hat with ribbons hanging down behind; when he pirouettes, beautifully starched white drawers are displayed.

The *Cherrero,* literally 'Pig-Man', and *Gatuzain* literally 'Cat-Man', also wear the traditional dance costume and scarlet bérets. The former has sheep-bells round his waist and in his hand a stick topped by a horse's tail with which he sweeps the ground at the head of the procession. The latter carries that same wooden spring trellis which we saw in the hands of the Austrian Fool, and which has been interpreted as a symbol of the lightning. Besides these the 'Reds' include a pair of Gelders and a number of Blacksmiths and *Kukulleros* all attendant on the Horse, and are accompanied by other characters including a Lord and Lady and a Peasant and Housewife.

The other group, the 'Blacks', are as dirty and dishevelled as the 'Reds' are neat and resplendent. They wear muddy boots in place of clean white *espadrilles*, and battered hats instead of the jaunty Basque béret. Occasionally they include a 'black' Hobby-horse, Standard-Bearer and *Cherrero* who parody their 'red' prototypes, but generally they consist only of Tinkers, Knife-Grinders and Gipsies

THE BASQUE MASCARADES

whose task it is to clear a space when it comes to dancing.

When the *Mascarades* are invited to visit a neighbouring village (to go uninvited is the deadliest of insults) they are met by the best dancers among their hosts and are obliged to pass a series of 'barricades', consisting of a rope drawn across the road or simply of two or three men armed with bottles and glasses. These can only be passed in the manner prescribed by tradition. The principal 'Reds' dance up to the barricade one after another and pass to the other side where a glass of wine awaits them, after which the 'Blacks' burst rowdily through. They then visit the village notables, dancing in their honour before their houses.

The best of the performance is reserved for the afternoon, and I will describe it as I saw it done by the men of Laguinge in their own tiny hamlet on Shrove Tuesday in 1930. The scene was a green meadow by a stream, and the background the white walls and slate roofs of the church and farm-houses clustered on the side of a hill. The performance was, as always, divided into two parts, the *Branle* and the *Fonctions.* The 'Blacks' cleared a space by running a cart round the circle of spectators, and after a couple of *Sauts Basques* the 'Reds' chose partners from among the village girls, who allowed themselves with a great show of resistance to be dragged into the circle, there to form a chain for what proved to be a very elaborate double *Farandole,* led by the Lord and the Peasant. First, however, came the *Gavotte* and the *Branli Haustia,* the former a figure dance to an old gavotte tune by the Hobby-horse, *Cantinière,* Sweeper and Fool, and the second culminating in a series of dazzling solo performances. The Lord and his partner held up a handkerchief as in *Oranges and Lemons,* and one by one the Standard-Bearer and the four dancers of the *Gavotte* danced up to it and in his honour displayed their most elaborate steps. The skill and virtuosity of these rustics were almost unbelievable. Their steps were those of the most accomplished ballet-dancers. Nothing came amiss to them, *brisés,* double beats, *cabrioles* and *entrechats.* Not content with the usual *entrechat quatre* in which the legs are simply crossed and uncrossed in the air, they went on to *entrechat huit* and *dix.* Nearly two feet into the air shot the tense muscular bodies, and seemed to hang for a moment suspended while the twinkling feet crossed and recrossed two and even three times before dropping lightly back to earth. This part concluded with the *Snail Dance,* in which the two serpentine chains were wound by the Standard-Bearer into the tightest of spirals.

Hitherto the 'Blacks' had been little more than onlookers. Their turn came in the physiological sounding *Fonctions,* which consist of a series of dances and burlesque knockabout scenes, most of which we have not the space to describe. Two of them, however, are of real importance, for they form the culminating point of all *Mascarades,* and the first if not the second is always displayed whenever the Soule dances are exhibited. This is the famous *Godalet Dantza* or *Wineglass Dance,* which must be seen to be believed. A short tub glass half full of red wine was planted firmly on the ground in the middle of the circle, and the Sweeper danced out to do his steps, the showy steps of the *Branli Haustia,* round, over and all about the glass. As he finished, the *Gatuzain* approached the glass with a coy, sidling movement and went through the same performance. Next came the Standard-Bearer and the *Cantinière,* each embroidering the step until the Hobby-horse danced out, saddle-cloth flying out like a ballet-skirt, the little mirrors on his crown twinkling in unison with his magic feet as they crossed and recrossed in the triple *entrechat,* while all the time his 'mount' was curvetting and rearing and describing rhythmic circles all around and about the glass.

A second time these ballet-dancers, who were mountain shepherds, sabot-makers or wood-cutters, circled round the glass. This time, as each ended his steps, his foot began to feel for the glass itself. Gently, the ball of the foot was placed upon it; gently the weight of the body was shifted to that foot, until the dancer was standing on the glass. Then, even more delicately, he sprang into the air and alighted cleanly on the ground, the wine rocking, but not a drop spilling over. Now the Horse began his final round. The audience leant forward holding its breath, for this *tour de force* must be performed by touch and balance alone, the glass being hidden from the dancer by his cumbrous equipment. But no matter. Up he went, and stood there poised above his retinue like some Minoan ritualist with slender waist and plumed head-dress. Then, bringing us sharply back into the Christian era, he sketched the Sign of the Cross with his free foot, and with a miraculous bound sprang clear.

The Horse was again the central figure of the last of the *Fonctions*. The two Gelders, in black velveteens and gaiters, danced into the circle, arms round each other's necks. Round the ring they went to their own traditional tune, and then executed a burlesque dance with stick-tapping, hand-clapping and slapping as in some of the central European dances. Presently the Wineglass tune was again heard, and the Horse danced on. The Gelders approached, making pretence to entrap him, and finally with the aid of the Tinkers he was caught, shod by the Smiths and then gelded in mime. All his strength left him, and sinking down exhausted he staggered round the circle supported by his captors. Gradually, however, his forces seemed to return. Drawing himself up he began to leap into the air, his hands resting on the shoulders of the escort, until his final leap was so prodigious that it became a veritable hoisting, and for an instant he appeared in all his splendour above the heads of the crowd.

It would be no exaggeration to say that the union of traditional dance and mime finds its apogee in the Basque Masquerade. In this one performance are incorporated all the principal forms of both. The choreography includes the Processional, the Country dance, the Chain dance, the Spectacular dance and the Ritual dance. The principal figures have all the character of Morris men, and the attendants on the Horse carry little sticks suggesting that they were once Sword dancers. There is also the familiar opposition between two different groups of dancers and, in the 'barricades', some trace of mimic combat. The Horse is shod, and his exhaustion through gelding and subsequent recovery approximate to a resurrection. Apart from this, within comparatively recent times, the Knife-Grinders were accompanied by a Barber who cut the Master-Grinder's throat and a Doctor who revived him; the Tinker's wife gave birth to a baby on the stage (as I have also seen in a Portuguese mumming-play); and the Bear, who figures in many European mummings which we have not had the space to describe, also made his appearance.

In this one performance, therefore, are combined almost all the elements of dance and mime which we have had occasion to consider in this book. Might it not accordingly be thought that so complete a performance would help us to reconstitute some original norm of which less elaborate observances are but variants? Such, unfortunately, is not the case. The Basque Masquerade is rather to be regarded as the agglomeration of a number of different features of different origin and development. All these have been described in this book, and we have put forward tentative theories of their origin and interpretation. Such theories, however, cannot go beyond the realm of speculation and conjecture, for we are not dealing with an exact science in which causes can be deduced infallibly and with mathematical precision from their effects.

We are accordingly faced with a series of facts from which the inferences to be drawn must be left to individual judgement. If, in the four corners of our continent, we find people doing strikingly similar dances in association with strikingly similar customs on strikingly similar occasions, must we ignore the implications of these facts, or with unimaginative scepticism dismiss them as pure coincidence? May we not rather attempt to systematize the factors which are common to them and build up a hypothesis which will be consistent with them?

In this book we have adopted the latter course, well aware that we can argue only by analogy. We admit freely that our conclusions cannot be proved. One thing, however, is certain. Through all these dances runs a strain of earnest purpose, of ancient, atavistic instinct, working itself out in the actions of the dancers, and leaving the most critical spectator convinced that whatever their subsequent history, they sprang originally from the vast issues of Life and Death.

INDEX

PRINTED BY
NORTHUMBERLAND PRESS LIMITED
NEWCASTLE UPON TYNE